stampartistry

stampartistry

Combining Stamps with Beadwork, Carving, Collage, Etching, Fabric, Metalwork, Painting, Polymer Clay, Repoussé, and More

GLOUCESTER MASSACHUSETTS

ROCKPORT PUBLISHERS

ricë freeman~zachery

First published in the United States of America by
Rockport Publishers, Inc.
33 Commercial Street
Gloucester, Massachusetts 01930-5089
Telephone: (978) 282-9590
Fax: (978) 283-2742
www.rockpub.com

Library of Congress Cataloging-in-Publication Data
Freeman-Zachery, Ricë.
    Stamp artistry : combining stamps with beadwork, carving, collage, etching, fabric, metalwork, painting, polymer clay, repoussé, and more / Ricë Freeman-Zachary.
        p.   cm.
    ISBN 1-59253-011-7 (pbk.)
    1. Rubber stamp printing. I. Title
TT867.F74 2003
761—dc21

2003009398
CIP

ISBN 1-59253-011-7

10 9 8 7 6 5 4 3 2

Design: Mary Ann Guilette
Layout: Laura Herrmann Design
Photographer: Bobbie Bush Photography, www.bobbiebush.com
Illustrator: Judy Love
Project Manager/Copyeditor: Livia McRee
Proofreader: Stacey Ann Follin

Printed in China

To my husband, Earl, whose support, encouragement, and enthusiasm make everything possible.

CONTENTS

INTRODUCTION

Rubber stamping has come a long, long way since the early days, when there was a handful of stamp companies and only one publication. When I first got involved with stamping and began writing for *Rubberstampmadness*, the granddaddy of all the stamping magazines, my "hobby" was almost unheard of. In the years since, stamping has not so much changed as expanded. There are still those of us who have vintage stamps from the early days, especially our treasured alphabet sets and funky, quirky images—and we use them just as we did decades ago, stamping letters and decorating envelopes to send through the mail. Now, though, there are entirely new areas of stamping, replete with thousands of new images and scores of modern inks that allow us to stamp on everything from plastic to metal and almost every surface in between.

Even more exciting than all the new products available today is the work of artists who've discovered stamping and have found ways to incorporate it into the art they create. Metal artists find innovative ways to stamp on metal. Silk artists use stamps to make art on silk. Jewelry artists incorporate stamping into their jewelry making. This experimentation has blurred the line between rubber stampers and artists and has made stamping a legitimate art technique.

In this book, you'll find projects that incorporate stamping in new ways; you'll be able to create clothes, jewelry, and home accents that are miles away from the old standards. You'll see names you recognize from classes, workshops, and galleries, artists who make assemblages and clothing and jewelry—all of them using rubber stamping in their work. These artists started out working as dress designers, silk painters, and metal workers; now they're doing all those things and using rubber stamps in the process, creating eye-popping art for every facet of your life.

In "For the Home," you'll find functional art for the space where you live, including a funky painted-and-stamped Lazy Susan and canvas-covered hangers for your wearable art, which you'll be making day and night once you've seen the pieces in "For the Body."

"For the Body" focuses on art you can wear, from elegant silk shawls to funky denim skirts. Fill those hangers—and your closet—with these, and all you'll need are accessories, such as the oh-so-glamorous purse made from a cigar box—you've seen

them in boutiques for way more than you wanted to spend. Now you can make your own, embellishing it with abandon.

Don't forget the jewelry. In "For the Jewel Box," you'll find instructions for all things ornamental, from metal bracelets to polymer clay brooches. And we're willing to wager that this is rubber-stamped jewelry like you haven't seen it before—pieces that you can wear proudly and pass down through generations.

If you're looking for a gift—either for a friend or for yourself—"For the Heart" has something for you. Have you ever seen those little Formica samples at the home improvement store and wondered what you could do with them? We'll teach you how to make them into key chains—some funky, some elegant, all perfect for giving.

Talismans and amulets, journals and shrines—all the kinds of things that nurture your spirit—are featured in "For the Soul." Here you'll find leather book covers for your art journals, amulet bags to hold secret treasures, and art dolls stamped with inspirational words to encourage creativity.

"For the Family" is all about ways to incorporate family photos into stamped projects. If you love using your photos in the art you create but don't like the look of just sticking a photograph into a stamped frame, these pieces are for you. We show how to use vintage photos on fabric and how to incorporate good-quality color copies into stamped work, so seamlessly joining the two that the photos look like part of the stamping. You'll also learn what you can do with photographs made into actual rubber stamps.

No matter what kind of art you're into—from metal work to altering your clothing—there's something here to inspire you, to delight you, to have you looking at your collection of stamps in a whole new way.

enjoy!

THE BASICS

The actual act of stamping—using a rubber stamp to make an image on a surface—is about as simple as any activity can be. You can vary the materials—the kinds of stamps and varieties of inks and materials receiving the image—to create a myriad of projects, and that's what we do here. Once you understand the basics of inking the stamps and creating the images, you'll be well on your way.

KINDS OF RUBBER STAMPS

You can buy stamps, have your art converted into rubber or photopolymer stamps, or carve your own stamps. They all work in basically the same way. In addition to these obvious stamps, there are all kinds of other materials that can be used for stamping. In the prequel to this book, *The Stamp Artist's Project Book,* Sharilyn Miller describes how to use a multitude of these materials, from bubble wrap to cut-up fruit to Styrofoam plates.

INKS AND PAINTS

Although most stamped images are created using either ink or paint, you can, in practice, use any of an amazing variety of liquids to get an image onto a substrate. You can stamp with food coloring and icing, or with dyes and bleach. The only way to know what will and won't work is to experiment with everything. Standard inks are a little more mundane but are tried and true and a good place to start:

- DYE INK—This is the most common stamp ink and has been around the longest. Once found only in office supply stores and limited to blue, black, red, and (maybe) green, dye ink can now be found in every shade you can imagine, as well as in multicolored rainbow pads. This ink is fugitive, sensitive to both water and light; it will run and blur if it gets wet, and it will fade away over time.

- PERMANENT DYE INK—This ink, like regular dye-based inks, is absorbed into the substrate. The difference is that it's been manufactured to stay put. In some cases, it needs to be heat-set. Check the individual ink for directions about heat-setting and information about whether that particular ink is lightfast.

- PIGMENT INK—These inks are slightly thicker than dye-based inks and dry on the surface of the substrate (rather than being absorbed). They tend to produce more vividly-colored images than dye inks and many are more permanent. As always, do test stampings to make sure how each one reacts.

- PERMANENT PIGMENT INK—This is often called heat-set crafter's ink. Like regular pigment ink, it dries on top of the surface; once you set it with a heat tool, it's permanent. Again, there are degrees of permanence, so test first.

- EMBOSSING INK—This ink is designed to stay wet and hold the embossing powder to the substrate until you melt the powder with a heat tool.

- SPECIALTY INKS—You can now buy inks made to stamp on almost any surface, from glass to metal. Read the directions carefully and follow all guidelines completely, and always do a test stamping on the exact material you plan to use. The ink that you want to use may not be one that's marketed for the kind of stamping you do. My favorite ink for stamping on fabric is sold for screen-printing. I've never screen-printed in my life, but a call to Dharma Trading Company with a question about an ink that would be truly permanent on fabric elicited the suggestion that I try this ink. I did, and I'm very happy with it—which goes to prove that it's personal experience and experimentation that leads you to the perfect ink for your projects.

- PAINT—There are a lot of different kinds of paint, and you can stamp with many of them, depending on the surface you're stamping. Acrylic paints are good for stamping on coated or painted surfaces, such as the base-painted Lazy Susan on pages 30 and 31. Parts of Susan Lenart Kazmer's "Found Object Talisman Bracelet" (pages 74 and 75) were stamped with fingernail polish.

iNKING

There are several ways to ink your rubber stamps. The most basic is to press the rubber onto the surface of a stamp pad. For larger stamps, you can lay the stamp faceup on a flat surface and pat the ink pad onto the rubber, moving the ink pad, rather than the stamp, to get even coverage. You can also use a rubber brayer to ink larger stamps; roll the brayer several times over the ink pad, and then roll the brayer onto the rubber to transfer the ink.

STaMPING THe IMaGE

Once your stamp is inked, you're ready to stamp on a surface. Press the inked rubber to the paper or wood or whatever—straight down, with firm, even pressure. Don't rock the stamp back and forth; this can cause the image to blur. Lift straight up. That's it—unless you're stamping on a curved surface or around the corner of, say, a wooden box. In those cases, you'll need to practice. For curved surfaces, roll the stamp around the curve, never letting it slide. Practice keeping part of the stamp in contact with part of the surface at all times. For stamping around a corner, practice on small cardboard boxes to find out if it's easier for you to stamp with the box or the stamp lying on a flat surface, in which case you have to manipulate only one or the other.

EMBOSSING

If you want to emboss, the most important consideration is the ink. The most common problem with embossing when you first begin stamping is trying to emboss using regular ink. Some inks—especially dye ink—do not stay wet long enough to hold the embossing powder on the surface. You need an ink that stays wet, holding the powder until you melt it with a heat tool. Although some pigment inks work fine for this, your best bet is to use ink specially designed for embossing. Stamp your image with this ink. Pour the embossing powder onto the wet image; you needn't try for exact placement—you can just dump the powder onto the surface. Then pour off the excess onto scrap paper and funnel it back into the container. After that, use a heat tool or heat gun to heat the powder until it melts. Experimentation will show how long to heat it and from what distance—different powders melt at different rates. You don't want the powder to get so hot that it bubbles, unless the bubbly look is what you're after. Again: experimentation is the key!

Now that you have your image stamped, you can do all kinds of things with it.

aDDING COLOr TO STaMPED ImaGES

If you've stamped on paper, you can add color with pencils, chalks, markers, crayons, watercolors, paints, or inks. On wood, you can use many of the same colorants: soft-lead colored pencils work especially well on very smooth, soft wood, such as basswood. For substrates like metal and glass, you can color with the same kind of inks or paints that you use for stamping. Use a little of the ink or paint in a palette or tiny plastic cup, and apply it to the desired areas of the image with a small brush, cotton swab, or even your finger. On fabric, the colorant you use depends on how permanent you want it to be. For fabric that won't be washed, such as that used in the photo transfer pin on pages 112 and 113, you can color the stamped images with colored pencils; just be careful not to rub the colored areas. If you're going to wash the fabric, you can color with diluted fabric paint or stamping ink. My favorite is fabric crayons or fabric

dye sticks; these waxy sticks go on dry, allowing me to put color exactly where I want it. You can use fabric markers, too. As always when working with fabric that will be washed, remember to heat-set everything (see Stamping on Fabric, pages 17 to 20).

MASKING

Masking is one of the most useful techniques for stamping. You can use it on any surface, with any stamp. It allows you to stamp part of an image, to make one image appear to lie behind another, and to overlap images. To mask, you'll stamp an image twice: once on the surface where you want it and once on scrap paper. Cut out the scrap paper stamping, cutting just on the inside of the line. Not way inside—you want it just a fraction of a millimeter smaller than the real image. Apply a little temporary adhesive to the back of the cut-out image, and lay it exactly over the real one. Then stamp another image over part of the first, masked image. Remove the mask, and the second image appears to have been stamped behind the first one. You can layer as many images as you like by using masks, and you can create complicated scenes. You can use it with other techniques, like photo transfers—check out the brooch on pages 58 and 59. I ironed on the image of me as a kid. When I peeled off the paper, I saved it to use as a mask, laying it back over the transfer before stamping the wings. This is a great way to use stamps with transfers; you can add wings, crowns, and all kinds of accessories to your photos on fabric.

EMBELLISHING

There are so many embellishments for stamping that there's really no way to cover them all. Where we once had glitter glue and stickers, we now have everything from colored eyelets to metal tags, all marketed to rubber stampers and available in most stamp stores. You can find tags in every color and shape, letters in materials from plastic to metal to glass, and almost anything else you can think of—and that's just the embellishments that are meant to be used with stamping. If you go further afield and look at all the other possibilities, you'll find washers and nuts at the hardware store, grommets and buttons at the fabric store, parchment paper and foil at the grocery store. Once you begin looking at everything with what I call "a stamping eye," you'll see embellishments everywhere. The only problem will be finding a way to store everything you collect.

GLUES

You can never have too many kinds of glue, and it's imperative that you have the right kind for whatever project you're working on. Glue sticks meant for paper-to-paper gluing won't work for metal pieces, and the cement you use for metal work will soak right through fabric. If you're going to be stamping on all kinds of materials, you'll want to have a minimum of a half dozen adhesives:

- a good glue stick for paper
- collage glue that will let you glue paper to paper without buckling and wrinkling—you can also use this as a sealer over the finished collage
- thick white glue for attaching porous embellishments, such as fabric flowers
- glue for nonporous surfaces, such as metal-to-metal gluing

- a fabric glue stick for temporarily attaching things to fabric until you can sew them in place
- permanent, washable fabric glue—I don't trust this enough to use it by itself, without sewing, but for rhinestones or other nonsewable trimmings, this is what you'll need
- wood glue; in many cases, thick white glue will work with wood

CLEANING YOUR STAMPS

Always clean your stamps as soon as you're finished for the day or you switch from stamping with ink to stamping with paint. If you let ink and paint dry on the rubber, it will clog the fine lines in the images, and eventually you will be able to print only partial images. The best way to clean most ink from rubber stamps is by stamping on a wet paper towel. If the ink is permanent, you'll need stamp cleaner designed for that ink; most stamp companies sell stamp cleaner designed to remove specific inks from rubber stamps. For acrylic paint and fabric paint, you'll need a little mild soap mixed with warm water. Use an old toothbrush to scrub the rubber. If you immerse wood-mounted stamps in water, sooner or later the rubber will come off the wood mount. For this reason, I like using a carved eraser alphabet for stamping words on fabric—I can just dump all the letters into a sink of warm, soapy water and let them soak until I have time to scrub them with a toothbrush.

Protect your rubber stamps by keeping them away from heat and sunlight. Don't use harsh or oily chemical cleaners on them. With a little common sense care, your stamps should last for years and years.

TECHNIQUES

Although the best way to learn is to play with your materials and experiment with everything, it's always nice to have the benefit of someone else's experience. The talented artists featured in this book have been experimenting for years and have perfected a variety of techniques that are sure to enhance your rubber stamping.

ERASER CARVING

It began with artists carving images on actual erasers, using a craft knife and limiting the size of the image to what would fit on one of those crumbly pink erasers. Things have changed, and now you can buy carving blocks in any size, even huge sheets. You can carve with a craft knife or a linoleum cutter with interchangeable blades, or you can use a Dremel tool with a flexible shaft attachment and various fine bits to create intricate works. However you choose to carve, you'll first need to get the image onto the block. Remember that the stamp will be a mirror image of your original design. If you draw on the block, remember to reverse letters and words.

To transfer photocopies to carving material, you'll need a fresh copy and something containing acetone: fingernail polish remover works well, but you can also buy blender markers or just the acetone itself (from a hardware store). The fumes are harmful, so make sure to do the transfers either outdoors or in a room with excellent ventilation. Place the copy facedown on the carving block. Saturate a cotton ball or small piece of fabric with the acetone, and let that saturate the back of the copy. Rub the paper firmly with the bowl of a spoon or something similarly solid. Lift an edge of the paper, and check to see if the toner has transferred. If not, replace the paper and repeat.

Do a lot of tests as you're carving, stopping to stamp and check every once in a while to make sure your image is forming the way you want it to. It's better to remove too little of the material at first; you can always go back and cut away more.

Finally, remember that just because you're making a carving of an image, it doesn't mean that you can use other people's drawings or photographs without permission. Use either your own drawings or clip art to make sure you're not violating any copyright restrictions.

eraser carving

STAMPIMG ON WOOD

Stamping on wood is one of the most versatile of techniques, as varied as the kinds of wood surfaces on which you might want to stamp: raw wood, smooth unfinished wood, polished wood, painted wood. Each wooden surface requires a different approach and, often, different media.

Untreated wood is porous, and that's important to consider. Raw wood—wood that hasn't been sealed or coated—will absorb some of whatever you put on it. If you stamp with dye-based inks, some of those inks will soak into the surface of the wood. Sometimes you may want that effect, but often you'll want to prevent it by using pigment inks. The best stamping inks for most unfinished wooden surfaces are heat-set, permanent pigment inks. I've had success with regular pigment inks, though, so I recommend experimenting to see what works best on your project. Stamp on the bottom of the piece or on the inside. Let the ink dry, heat-set it if necessary, and then add color (if your project calls for this) and rub it to see if it's going to smear. You can always sand these test stampings off of raw wood; so go ahead and see what happens when you use a particular ink on your particular wood.

For finished or sealed wood you'll need an ink or paint that will dry on a nonporous surface, or you'll need to remove the finish. You can do this with sandpaper or a wood stripper; it depends on how thick the finish is and how much effort you want to spend

on it. Sanding away worn or roughened finishes isn't difficult, but it's tough to sand off all of a good, solid sealer; for that, you'll probably want to use a stripper. Choose one that's nontoxic, if possible. Sand the wood after you've stripped it to remove any residue.

For wood painted with acrylics you can stamp with acrylic paint, just as long as the base paint hasn't yet been sealed. See Linda Woods' "Funky Lazy Susan" on pages 30 and 31 for details.

STAMPIMG ON POLYMER CLAY

Stamping on clay is great fun: it's a combination of playing with clay and stamping, and you can do all sorts of things with the two. New clays made with fine silver are available today, so you can create real silver pieces—perfect for stamped jewelry!

To prepare your clay, you need to condition it. This means softening it up enough to roll out and use; many clays are so firm and uncooperative that they're almost impossible to work with until you've softened them a lot. You can do this in several ways. Some artists lay the package of clay under a heating pad, and some actually sit on it. You can warm it in your hands, and that's usually best: warm it a little and then start rolling it and twisting it. As it begins to soften, this step will become easier until the clay is soft enough for you to roll out or run through a pasta machine that's strictly used for clay. Do *not* condition it by popping it into the oven or microwave.

The actual stamping on the clay is easy: press firmly, but not so firmly that the stamp goes all the way through the clay. You can do this with inked stamps or clean ones, depending on the effect you want. You can brush on metallic dust or pigments, and you can add color after baking the clay. The possibilities are endless. The only way to find out what results you like best is to get a bunch of clay and all your stamping supplies and experiment.

Additions to the stamping are a little more complicated—and a lot of fun. You've probably seen photos transferred onto clay. There are all kinds of ways to get pictures onto your unbaked clay piece, and there are new materials being developed all the time.

The easiest method is one that's available to anyone with access to a copy machine: make a good, dark photocopy, either black-and-white or color, of the photograph or clip art. Roll out light-colored clay. Trim the photocopy, and place it facedown on the clay. Press firmly in place without mashing the clay. Smooth the paper in place with a brayer. Leave the copy in place overnight. When you peel off the photocopy, the image will have transferred to the clay. Stamp it and bake it according to package directions, and you've got clay pieces you can use in all sorts of projects. The black-and-white copies have always worked better for me, but experimenting with various color copy machines will allow you to find what works best for you.

Bake your clay according to the directions on the package. The temperature and time will vary according to the kind of clay and the thickness of the piece you're making. If you're going to do a lot of clay work, invest in an oven thermometer so that you can get exact temperatures.

With polymer clay, you'll want to use a toaster oven that you use only for baking the clay and not for preparing food. Although the clay itself is nontoxic, the fumes produced by burning clay are, so make sure you have adequate ventilation—that means that you need fresh air coming into the room and a way for fumes to get out. If you need to sand the clay after it's baked, always use a dust mask—there's no need to take chances with fumes and dust.

stamping on polymer clay

METAL CLAY

Metal clay is wonderful stuff, and it opens up a whole new world of stamping on clay. Many of the same rules apply to both regular polymer clay and metal clay, with a few differences. Metal clay doesn't need to be conditioned before you work with it, but some brands will dry out within five minutes. Other brands stay workable longer; check the package for specifics. Metal clay must be fired, and it shrinks. You'll have to take this into consideration when you make jewelry, for example. You'll also have to dry the clay completely before you fire it. There are several ways to do this:

- Air dry the piece overnight.

- Place the stamped piece, on a Teflon sheet, in a toaster oven at 200°F (93°C) for 10 to 15 minutes.

- Place the piece in a food dehydrator at 165°F (74°C) for 20 to 25 minutes.

- Dry it with a hair dryer: cut a hole the size of the hair dryer nozzle in the bottom of a cardboard box that is approximately 12" (30.5 cm) deep. Place the nozzle snugly through the hole so that the nozzle extends into the box. Open the top of the box, then place the clay piece on a heat-resistant surface and put the box over it. Turn the dryer on high. Although drying time will vary according to the type of hair dryer, the size of the box, and the size of the clay piece, it should take about 5 to 10 minutes. Check the piece for dryness by placing it on a mirror for a minute or two. Pick up the piece and look at the mirror; if there is no fogginess, the piece is dry.

Metal clay must be fired, either in a kiln or with a butane microtorch, or—with some brands—on the burner of a gas stove. Firing requires all the care you'd take with anything that gets hot enough to effect metal. If you use a kiln, always turn it off before placing items in it or taking them out. Wear nonflammable clothing with short sleeves and no dangling fabric, and pull back your hair.

The color of fired silver clay is not superficial; it is the reflection of peaks and valleys in the metal. Brushing levels the peaks and valleys for a satin finish.

STAMPIMG ON FABRIC

You can stamp on all kinds of fabric, from cotton muslin to synthetics, as long as you use ink or paint designed for that fabric. Natural fibers—like the cotton and silk used in the "For the Body" chapter—are the most common and are the easiest to work with.

Stamping on fabric is one of my favorite techniques; one of the things I like to do most is to stamp on aged, old-looking fabric. Tea-dying is the easy way to get this great vintage look. And it's not limited to fabric; with a little care, you can tea-dye paper, card stock, and envelopes.

metal clay

stamping on fabric

Although you can purchase packets of dye for tea-dying, it's simple enough to use the real thing, and the results are much more interesting. You'll need a big, old pot (one that you don't mind staining), a lot of family-sized tea bags, and a stove. Fill the pot mostly full of water and dump in 4–6 large tea bags, and let it boil. Watch for splatters—boiling tea can make a mess. Some of the bags will tear apart; this is fine. When the tea has reached a deep, dark brown, add your material. If you're dying paper, you want the dye to be very dark so that you don't have to leave the paper in too long: it will disintegrate. You want to be able to dip it in for a moment and then take it out. Check the color, and remove the pieces as soon as they're stained. Lay them on layers of newspaper to dry. If there are

darker areas that you don't blot, they will create an interesting pattern when dry. Alternately, you can spoon the tea dye onto the paper—this works better with fragile paper. The downside is that you won't get that warped, worn look to go with the tea-stained color. I like to wad up my paper, envelopes, or tags, and then dump them in the pot for about 30 seconds. Take them out, lay them flat, and then spoon more dye on them. Also, try mixing instant coffee and hot water (a ratio of $1/4$ to 1 works well) and spooning it over the wet paper; sprinkle some dry coffee crystals on the paper for mottled effects.

You can leave fabric in the dye as long as you want, adding more water as necessary. You can put the fabric in dry or wet: dry fabric, wadded into a ball, will dye unevenly, with interesting color variations. If you wet the fabric first and dye it in smaller pieces that can be turned in the water, you'll get more even coloring. Experiment to find out which you like best. Try different kinds of teas for different shades of staining, or try the coffee mixture.

Rinse the dyed fabric and hang outside to dry to avoid staining your dryer. If you don't want to lose any of the stain, don't rinse the fabric and iron it until dry between old sheets on an old ironing-board cover.

To stamp on fabric, you'll need paint or ink that's permanent when laundered. This can range from stamping ink designed for fabric (not all are permanent) to acrylic paint (stiffens your fabric) to fabric paint (sometimes too thick for detailed stamps) to screen printing ink, which is my personal favorite. The only way to know which will work best for you is, again, to experiment. The results you get will depend on many factors, from the contents of the fabric to whether you stamp with the fabric dry (for crisp images) or damp (for softer, watercolor-like images).

One way to approach fabric stamping is to find things you can use on fabric that correspond with what you'd use on paper. Spray-on dye is like a chalk pastel background or a sponged background. You can use fabric markers just as you would markers designed for paper. Try fabric crayons the way you'd use regular ones. And for image transfers, you've got to try iron-on fabric transfers (see next section).

The main thing to remember is to heat-set everything—and to heat-set it thoroughly. A quick tumble in the dryer isn't enough. Although most products intended for fabric carry their own instructions for heat-setting, most aren't very thorough. Over the years, I've combined several to come up with what I use. First, do not rely on your home dryer; it doesn't get hot enough.

Allow the ink or paint to dry. Dry it at least overnight. I usually let mine dry for 48 hours. Preheat your iron to the maximum temperature for your particular fabric. Iron each section thoroughly; this means at least a minute or two for each stamped image. Move the iron in a circle while you're doing this so you don't scorch the fabric. For really thorough heat-setting, you can place a piece of aluminum foil on the ironing board and put the stamped side of the fabric on this foil; press the hot iron against the back side of the fabric.

IRON-ON TRANSFERS

Iron-on transfer has to be one of my very favorite things to do with stamping and fabric. All you need is a computer, scanner, and printer (or access to a color copy machine, iron-on transfers sheets, and an iron). You can transfer detailed stamp collages you create on paper and transfer them to fabric, and you can add photos to your stamped clothing.

Here's what you'll do: scan whatever you want, and print out the mirror image on transfer paper. Experiment with different kinds to find out what works best for you. Cut out the images, and heat up the iron to the hottest setting you can use on your fabric; keep in mind that transfers to cotton work best.

Now comes the important part. Most iron-on transfer sheets today are "cold peel," meaning that you iron the paper to the fabric, let it cool, and then peel off the paper backing, leaving the image in place. They used to be "hot peel," meaning you ironed and then peeled immediately, while the paper was still very, very hot. However, that caused a lot of burns, so now most sheets are cold peel. The problem is the image is rubbery, shiny, and slick when you peel the paper off. You may like this effect, but it's nothing like real fabric—it really changes the hand of the fabric you're using. Some sheets will allow you to hot peel, even though they say cold peel, but even if they don't, there's a solution.

iron-on transfer

Go ahead and do the cold peel, and then put a piece of waxed paper over the image and iron again, really heating up the image, moving your iron around until the whole thing is hot. What you're doing is melting the image—which is on a kind of plastic coating—into the fabric. Lift the waxed paper as soon as you stop ironing. You may have to repeat this a couple of times.

Some of the image may stick to the waxed paper—again, you have to experiment to find what works best with your fabric, your iron, and your particular brand of transfer paper. I use both Canon (more expensive but reliable) and Burlington (cheaper and pretty darned good) transfer sheets, and both can be peeled hot, even though the instructions say they're cold peel. I get the best results with cold peel and waxed paper.

After you've stamped your fabric and added the transfers, you can add other embellishments, just as you would to paper. There are all kinds of trims, buttons, and eyelets that will work marvelously on fabric and will go through the laundry. Play around and see what you like.

soldering

METAL

I really like stamping on metal because it's permanent: you can make something that will last, rather than something that will tear, fall apart, or fade away. There are a couple of basic techniques that will allow you to do amazing things with rubber stamps and metal.

If the possibilities intrigue you, check out your local rubber stamp store for more information. Ask about classes offered locally, or contact any of the artists who travel to teach at festivals and conventions.

SOLDERING Sandwiching a stamped paper collage between glass or between a piece of glass and a thin metal background allows you to protect the paper. I learned to solder from my dad; it's best if you get someone to let you watch and see how they hold the solder and the soldering iron. However, the basics are simple:

Apply copper tape to the edges you want to solder. Burnish it in place. Use an old brush to apply paste flux to the area to be soldered. Heat your soldering tool (you need one that will get hot but not too hot—I have a super-duper soldering gun that I can't use for this technique because it burns the paper through the glass). Let the soldering tool heat the copper tape, and touch the tip of the solder to the tape, moving along the edge.

stamping on metal

That's what they say to do. In practice, though, you'll have to find out what works best for you. I usually end up touching the tip of the soldering iron to the solder; I hold the solder with needle-nosed pliers. I anchor my glass in a small vise with a suction bottom that I can attach to the countertop; those and "third hand" devices, with alligator clips, are indispensable. At first it's awkward, trying to hold the piece of art, the solder, and the soldering iron. After some practice, though, it gets easier.

You can buy a solder that has lead in it. I don't; I use the lead-free kind. Also, get the solder without flux: if you buy the flux separately and apply it with an old brush, you can put it where you want it, giving you more control.

The best thing to do is to take a class and have someone show you how to solder. Some of the artists here teach classes where they include soldering. Donna Goss, who created the soldered charms on pages 64 and 65, is one. Check the artists' biographies for others who teach metal techniques (pages 136 and 137).

STAMPING ON METAL You can stamp on metal with permanent ink or paint. Dr. Ph. Martin markets several that are spectacular. Check Resources on pages 138 and 139 for contact information. Susan Lenart Kazmer sometimes stamps on metal with fingernail polish. Although it will eventually scrap off if not sealed, it gives you a great choice of colors and finishes. See the "Found Object Talisman Bracelet" on pages 74 and 75 for more ways to combine stamping and metal.

ETCHING ON METAL One very satisfying technique that Linda and Opie O'Brien and Susan Lenart Kazmer use to stamp a lot of their metal jewelry is metal etching. You'll need a metal etching solution called ferric chloride, which you can buy from Radio Shack as "PCB Etchant Solution." Stamp the metal with permanent ink, put masking tape over the back of the metal to protect it, and place it in the solution for at least two hours, checking it every hour or so after that. The etching solution will eat away the part of the metal that's not protected by the ink. If you stamped a star, that star will be raised after the metal has soaked in the etching solution. Pretty cool, huh? Thoroughly wash off the etched metal, and you have a stamping that will last virtually forever.

As you can imagine, this technique is not for children. Anything that will eat through metal will do some damage if it's spilled, so use it carefully. Follow the manufacturer's directions, wear rubber gloves, make sure you have adequate ventilation to protect your lungs—and have fun!

etching on metal

FOR THE
HOME

Most artists make the bulk of their work for other people, either as gifts or as pieces to sell or exhibit. One of the great joys of making art is sharing it, but most of us spend all of our time creating work that we get to enjoy only briefly before we send it out into the world.

Making art for our home, whether it's functional art or purely decorative, is one way we can surround ourselves with what we love to create. Even if we have to convince ourselves that it's cheaper to make our own decorations than it is to buy them, we have the perfect reason to create with only ourselves, our family, and our home in mind. Never mind what's popular, what sells, what colors our best friend likes. It's about us and what makes us happy, what makes our souls sing when we come home at the end of a long day, and what makes us smile when we wake up in the morning.

On the following pages, you'll find art for your home that ranges from a wonderful stamped canvas to exquisite ornaments made from fine metal clay. If you want to stamp on the wooden lazy Susan in your kitchen or studio, we've got just the piece for you. If you need something to dress up your closet, you've come to the right place. Whether you want to make decorative art that lets you stamp on painted gourds or create a one-of-a-kind picture frame, this is the chapter for you. Open the door, turn the page, and you'll find an environment that's warm and welcoming and filled with art you'll love creating especially for the place you call "Home."

a clown's kiss

There's no reason why all your stamped creations should be confined to envelopes or the pages of your art journal. Make them large, on stretched canvases, and you can hang them on the walls of your home. This piece began with a postcard image of a clown; it is stamped with hand-carved and rubber art stamps and shapes cut from craft foam. The result? Art you'll be proud to display.

MATERIALS

- stretched canvas, approximately 8" × 16" (20.5 cm × 40.5 cm)
- clown postcard
- large manila tag
- gold thread
- black thread
- paper
- craft foam (we used Fun Foam)
- scissors
- brush
- permanent black ink
- sponge
- matte medium
- acrylic paints: sage, yellow, and black
- metallic gold paint
- art stamps
- large needle
- embellishments: beads, fibers, buttons, trim

1 Paint the canvas with the acrylic paints, and allow it to dry.

2 Apply black paint to a hand-carved stamp, and stamp across the top and bottom of the canvas. Allow this to dry. Use the metallic gold paint to stamp a second row of the tile, and then over-stamp the black images.

3 Cut a diamond shape from craft foam. Stamp the diamond in sage, and then over-stamp with gold.

4 Use the matte medium to adhere the clown postcard to the manila tag. Glue the tag lightly to the canvas, and then stitch it in place with the large needle threaded with both the gold and black thread.

5 Sponge acrylic paint onto scrap paper, and allow to dry. Stamp the harlequin pattern onto the painted paper, and allow to dry. From this paper, cut out a hat shape. Glue it over the top of the clown's head. Embellish the clown's hat with trim and beads as desired.

6 Use black ink to stamp a diamond border across the canvas. Stamp the border again on the painted scrap paper. Cut out the diamond shapes, and mount them over the stamped border.

DiRECTiONS FOr THe BaSE

1   Use white glue or the matte medium to glue decorative papers to the wood block, covering it completely. Stamp each side, using permanent black ink.

2   Dip the wooden discs and buttons or game tiles into walnut ink, and allow them to dry. Apply gold wax finish to the discs.

3   Glue the discs together and then to the top of the block, using strong adhesive. This is where your pen will fit. Glue the buttons or tiles to the bottom of the block for feet, and allow to dry.

"blockhead" penholder & pen

This whimsical pen and penholder set will replace that boring old wooden one or that cheesy plastic one that has been cluttering up your desk. Decorated with stamped images that reflect your personal taste, this set will inspire your writing and brighten up your life. As an added bonus, the ink cartridge can be removed and replaced, so the pen will last as long as you do.

DIRECTIONS FOR THE PEN

1 Condition the clay (see pages 15 and 16). Run the conditioned clay through a pasta machine on a medium setting, or roll it out with the roller to approximately $^1/_8$" (3 mm). This will form the base.

2 Remove the cap of the pen and take out the ink cartridge, using pliers if necessary. Wrap a piece of paper around the pen to make a pattern for the clay. The paper should cover the entire length of the white part of the pen body and should wrap all the way around the pen, with a slight overlap. It will be approximately $1^1/_8$" × $4^3/_4$" (2.75 cm × 12 cm). Set the template aside.

3 Make a cane by rolling each color of the clay through the pasta machine on the thinnest setting, one color at a time, and then layering them. Cut them into squares and stack them together, sandwiching gold leaf sheets between some of the layers.

4 Distress the stack by pressing things into its surface: bamboo sticks, pens, furniture casters—anything that will leave an impression in the clay, causing distortions in the stack. Use the clay blade to slice thin layers of the distressed clay, creating interesting patterns and designs. Place these layers on the clay base created in step 1. Run the decorated clay through the pasta machine to smooth out the designs.

5 Place the template over the smoothed clay, and cut around it. Roll the clay around the pen, and smooth the seam. Cover the cap end of the pen separately, making sure it's flat.

6 Bake the pen in the toaster oven according to package directions, approximately 20 minutes at 270°F (132°C). Either sand and polish the pen or apply the clay glaze, and allow to dry.

7 Cut the fibers, and thread them through the silver bead. Tie the fibers, and glue the bead to the top of the pen. Insert the ink cartridge into the pen, and replace the cap.

MATERIALS

for the pen:
- plain Bic pen
- polymer clay: several colors (we used Premo)
- gold leafing sheets
- scrap paper
- clay "tissue" blade
- silver bead with hole large enough to accommodate fibers
- assorted fibers in colors to coordinate with the clay
- clay glaze or buffing wheel
- pasta machine or roller
- needle-nosed pliers

for the holder:
- 2" (5 cm) square wooden block
- two 1" (2.5 cm) wooden discs with center holes
- 4 small wooden buttons or game pieces
- walnut ink
- assorted collage papers
- white glue and glue brush
- matte sealer
- black permanent ink
- art stamps
- gold wax finish (we used Rub 'n Buff)
- toaster oven
- strong adhesive (we used E6000)

rubber-stamped gourd vessels

These stamped vessels don't look as if they were made from gourds; they look like ancient clay pots. But gourds they are, and their transformation is easy to effect. Once transformed, they're perfect for holding an arrangement of dried grasses or flowers.

MATERIALS

- gourds in various sizes
- decorative wire
- art stamps
- embossing ink
- heat tool
- **stain** (either a liquid leather dye or a mixture of acrylic paint and water, diluted to consistency of a stain)
- **airbrush, markers, paint** (we used Modern Options paints)
- sandpaper
- hacksaw or jigsaw
- file
- awl
- acrylic paint
- sponge
- **soap** (Murphy's Oil Soap is recommended)
- plastic scrubber
- grapefruit spoon

1   Wash the gourd with soap and scrubber, and let it dry. Using the hacksaw or jigsaw, cut off the top of the gourd. Use the file to smooth the cut edge. With the awl, make holes around the edge about every $1/2$" (1.3 cm).

2   Scrape out all the seeds and pulp from the inside of the gourd. The grapefruit spoon works really well for this. Stain the inside of the gourd. You can use leather dye or a thin mixture of acrylic paint and water: brush on the paint, and then wipe it off with a paper towel.

3   Sand the outside of the gourd very lightly, taking care not to scratch the surface. Paint the outside of the gourd. Modern Options paints were used here and are recommended. Follow the excellent directions on the package if you use those. If not, you can add color with an airbrush or Copic markers and the airbrush attachment.

4   Use black pigment ink to stamp the images. Emboss them with clear embossing powder, and heat-set them.

5   Sponge on a little acrylic paint, very sparingly, to add subtle highlights.

6   Seal with a spray sealer. Allow it to dry.

7   Decorate the rim with wire wrapped through the holes.

TIPS

- *You can mix several shades of acrylic paint to get a color that matches your decor.*

- *After everything is dry, you can use strong adhesive to attach metal charms, such as gold stars or tiny milagro houses.*

funky lazy susan
Creating this lazy Susan is so easy that you'll be inspired to stamp companion pieces: a bread box, a cutting board, a recipe file. But don't limit yourself to wooden pieces for the kitchen—a lazy Susan is great for keeping everything on the bedside table at arm's reach or for organizing all the art supplies in your studio. You can use commercially available rubber stamps, carve your own, or try what this artist used: stamps cut from craft foam.

1   Lightly sand the wood to remove any sealer or paint.

2   Base paint the piece with acrylic paint, and allow it to dry.

3   Cut stamps from the craft foam. Create texture by lightly scratching the surface with the razor blade.

4   Use the brush to apply acrylic paint to the stamps. Stamp over the base paint. Allow the paint to dry thoroughly.

5   When the paint is completely dry, use black acrylic paint and the liner brush to outline the stamped images.

6   Take the lazy Susan outside, and seal it with 3 or 4 light coats of spray sealer, allowing each to dry before applying the next.

MATERIALS
○ wooden lazy Susan
○ craft foam or stamps
   (we used Fun Foam)
○ acrylic paint
○ paint brush
○ liner brush
○ sandpaper
○ spray sealer
○ razor blade

ARTIST: *Peggy M. Koop*

silver pincushion

Since the advent of clays combined with precious metals, artists have been finding new ways to use the material. Combining the clay with rubber stamping opens a whole new realm of possibilities for stampers, jewelers, and home decorators.

MATERIALS

- 10 grams Art Clay Silver paste
- 10 grams Art Clay Silver syringe with tip
- 4-mm round-cut manmade gemstones
- silk or velvet fabric
- cotton ball
- cork clay
- textured art stamp
- straight pins with pearl ends
- needle and thread
- Teflon sheet
- artist's paintbrush
- small metal files
- stainless-steel brush
- contact cement
- burnishing tool
- polishing cloth
- small kiln (or access to a kiln)
- oxidizing agents, such as liver of sulfur or silver black (optional)
- fine silver bail back (optional)
- 18" (45.5 cm) ribbon (optional)

1 Mold cork clay into the shape of a shoe, forming the toe piece separately. This can be done by rolling a small amount of the clay into a ball and pressing it gently into the top of the shoe base, shaping it, and then removing it to dry separately. Dry both pieces slowly and thoroughly (see page 17). It is imperative that the cork clay be completely dry before proceeding to the next step.

2 Using the artist's brush, slowly fold (as when folding cake batter) the silver paste in the jar to a creamy consistency. Hold the clay shoe form that you've made by the top and bottom, and apply silver clay paste onto the sides and heel. Dry thoroughly as in step 1. Repeat for the bottom of the shoe, and dry.

3 Repeat for the top of the shoe, but apply paste from the heel to about 1/4" (6 mm) from the end of the toe. Do not paste over the end of the toe so that air can escape as the cork clay burns away during firing.

4 Apply paste, as described above, 4 to 6 more times or until the shoes begins to feel heavy in your hand. After applying the final layer of clay, press a rubber stamp lightly into the wet clay to texturize, and then dry as above.

5 Place the cork clay toe form back on top of the shoe tip. Some of the silver paste that you have already applied on the top of the shoe will extend under the cork clay toe form. Now, apply silver paste to the top and sides of the toe form, as described for the shoe form. The paste needs to overlap a little onto the bottom pieces so that the shoe is seamless. Texturize with the rubber stamp, and dry thoroughly.

6 With the syringe of silver clay, apply a small circle of clay to accommodate the 4-mm gemstones. Press the gemstones into the center of each circle. Dry thoroughly.

7 Use the metal files to file the uneven areas of the shoe before you fire it. File the bottom of the shoe so that it stands up on its own.

8 Place the shoe on fiberboard in the kiln, and fire at 1472°F (800°C) for 30 minutes. The cork clay will burn out during firing, leaving the shoe hollow. The inside tip of the toe will be open into the hollow form and will not be visible from the outside of the shoe. Brush the entire shoe with the stainless-steel brush, and burnish it to shine the raised areas of the texture.

9 Cut the fabric to fit the shoe sole, leaving 1/4" (6 mm) at the ends and 3/4" (18 mm) at the sides. Sew a running stitch around the edge of the fabric. Place about half of the cotton ball into the middle of the fabric, and gather the thread to form a shape that fits the shoe. Sew this closed.

10 Glue the stuffed shape into the shoe, using the contact cement, and allow to dry.

TiP

- *You can make the pincushion wearable by adding a bail back. Do this before firing the shoe. Use the syringe to apply a small bit of clay to the back of the shoe, and press the bail back into this clay. Add more clay to hide the ends of the bail back; dry thoroughly and fire. You can wear the pincushion on a ribbon threaded through the bail back.*

"expecting a miracle" picture frame

This frame combines several woodworking techniques: stamping on wood, wood burning, drilling, and staining. Starting with a plain, inexpensive wooden frame—available at any craft store—you can create a personalized shrine, fully colored and embellished. It's a great way to save and display mementos, like the milagros *shown here, that have a special meaning to you.*

1 Lightly sand the frame, and stain with the watercolors.

2 Stamp the image with permanent ink. Color with fluid acrylics and seal. Allow to dry.

3 Stamp the goddess on either basswood or foam board. The foam board is lighter and easier to cut out if you do not have a scroll saw. If you stamp on wood, burn over the image; then decorate with watercolors and markers, and apply sealer.

4 Drill holes and use wire to attach the goddess to a square of Masonite or foam board that has been cut to fit the frame and covered with the art paper.

5 Glue the vintage bingo card to the back of the frame.

6 Drill holes along the side and attach the *milagros* and beads with wire. Dangle one *milagro* from the other side.

MATERIALS

- unfinished wood frame, 5" × 7" (12.5 cm × 18 cm)
- coated wire
- beads
- *milagros*
- basswood (¼" [6 mm]) or foam board
- art stamps
- art paper
- glue
- Masonite or foam board
- bingo card
- fluid acrylics
- watercolor paint (we used Dr. Ph. Martin's Radiant Concentrated Watercolors)
- markers (Copic markers)
- wood sealer
- brushes
- drill
- fine sandpaper
- saw or cutting knife

TIPS

- *Embellish the frame with beads, charms, or vintage game pieces.*
- *Spell out words or a name with Scrabble tiles along the bottom edge.*

MATERIALS

- one sheet of 24-karat gold foil
- silver wire (at least 18-gauge)
- gold ribbon
- art stamp
- glue (use either rice glue or diluted white glue)
- agate burnisher
- neoprene rubber block
- plastic roller
- olive oil
- Teflon sheet
- two small strips framing matte board or 3 or 4 playing cards taped together
- craft knife
- small drinking straw
- fine-tip paintbrush
- dish of water
- hair dryer, toaster oven, or dehydrator
- small metal files
- stainless steel brush
- sandpaper (400-, 600-, 1200-, and 2000-grit)
- tweezers
- oxidizing agent such as liver of sulfur or silver black
- small kiln or access to a kiln
- long tweezers or tongs
- heat-resistant gloves
- polishing cloth
- silver polishing agent (use commercial polish or baking soda and a toothbrush)
- firing board or heat-resistant surface
- 1/2" (1.3 cm) wooden dowel
- small amount of dishwashing soap

stamped silver ornament

This ornament features a Santa face, but you're not limited to holiday ornaments. The technique of combining fine silver clay with 24-karat gold foil is a version of a Korean gold-foiling process called kumboo (pronounced koom-bow) and will allow you to create marvelous mixed-metal pieces using your favorite rubber stamps.

1   Apply a small amount of olive oil to your hands; then roll the silver clay into a ball. Place the ball on the Teflon sheet, with the matte board strips on either side. These strips will allow you to roll the clay to an even thickness of using the plastic roller.

2   Apply a little olive oil to the rubber stamp, and stamp the rolled-out clay. Press firmly, but not so firmly that the stamp goes all the way through the clay or makes an impression on the back. Use the craft knife to cut around the stamped impression. Use the small drinking straw to create a hole for hanging. Leave the ornament on the Teflon sheet, and dry it thoroughly using one of the methods on page 17.

3   When the ornament is completely dry, place it on the rubber block and use the metal files on any rough areas. Lightly sand the top with 1200-grit sandpaper, taking care not to sand away the stamped image. Smooth the back as much as possible for a high-mirror shine later.

4   Place the ornament on a heat-resistant firing board, and fire at 1600°F (871°C) for 10 minutes; then cool the ornament by holding it with tweezers and dipping it in cool water.

5   Brush the ornament both vertically and horizontally with the stainless-steel brush, both front and back, to bring out the satin finish.

6   Place the ornament on the rubber block (to prevent slippage), and put the block into a bowl of water (or under running water). Keep the ornament wet as you sand the top, bottom, and sides with the sandpaper. Start with 400 grit; then use 600, 1200, and 2000 grit, in that order. On the front, sand only the open, image-free areas. On the back, sand the entire surface to create a high-mirror shine.

7   Cut out small pieces of gold foil to fit into the face area and on the star. Apply glue with the paintbrush, and affix foil. Allow to dry.

8   Heat the kiln to 1600°F (871°C). Turn off kiln; wearing protective gloves, place the ornament into the kiln with tongs. Shut the door, and turn the kiln back on. Leave the ornament inside for two minutes at 1600°F (871°C). Turn off the kiln; wearing the gloves, open the door, and remove the ornament with tongs. Place the ornament on a heat-resistant firing block, and burnish the gold foil onto the silver with an agate burnisher. Allow to cool.

9 Brush and sand the ornament as in step 6, being careful not to brush or sand the gold-foiled areas.

10 Use the fine-tip paintbrush to apply oxidizing agent to the deep lines—in this case, the lines in the hat and beard. Be careful not to get any of the agent on the gold foil. Hold the ornament under cold running water with tongs to stop the oxidizing process. Avoid getting the oxidizing agent on your skin. Polish with silver polishing agent, again being careful not to get any on the gold foil. Clean with soap and water.

11 Attach the silver wire to the ornament. Make a small loop at the other end of the wire, and bend the wire over a wooden dowel to create a hanger. Attach the ribbon.

covered clothes hangers

Even the most decoratively dressed artist—the one whose every piece of clothing reflects her art—has a closet that needs help, stuffed with glorious clothes hanging on hangers that are, frankly, ugly. Even colored hangers or those cumbersome plastic things leave much to be desired, aesthetically speaking. Why can't hangers be lovely, reflecting the tastes of their owners? If you work in wearable art and your clothes are displayed in your workshop or studio, you want the hangers to be attractive, too. These hangers are fun to look at—and the canvas covers protect the shoulders of all your favorite artwear.

1 Carefully remove the paper from the hanger, and flatten it smooth to use as a template. Lay it on top of the canvas, and trace around it in pencil.

2 Cut out the canvas cover, and paint it with the base color. Allow to dry.

3 Use the sponge to apply paint to the rubber stamp, and stamp on the canvas. Allow to dry.

4 Following the creases on the paper template, fold the canvas cover over the hanger and glue the edges, securing them with clothespins if needed.

5 When the glue is dry, take the hanger outside and seal with spray sealer. Allow to dry thoroughly before using.

MATERIALS

○ dry-cleaning hanger with paper cover

○ canvas

○ acrylic paint

○ paint brush

○ stamps

○ sponges

○ tacky glues

○ spray sealer

○ pencil

○ scissors

○ see iris pattern, page 134

TIPS

- *If all your hangers are the same size, you can use the same paper template over and over, so that you don't have to buy hangers from a dry cleaner.*

- *Spray paint the hanger before covering; the hook will show, so you can have gold and silver hangers or hangers that match your clothes.*

- *You can jazz up your hangers even more by adding fibers and beads to the neck.*

FOR THE
BODY

Although wearable art has been around as long as people have been adorning their bodies, the idea of creating art to wear has seemed daunting to those who don't sew their own clothes. The artists in this section have embraced new techniques and materials and have designed exciting projects that allow anyone to create wearable works of art, even if their experience with the materials is limited. Although some of the featured projects are more involved and take some time to complete, all are within the range of moderately experienced crafters, and even the most complicated are designed for the nonprofessional.

You can create clothes ranging from the elegant—stamped silk shawls and ties—to the funky—altered jeans skirts and canvas shoes. You can also make purses to go with them—we'll show you how to make an elegant Cigar Box Purse and a stamped suede carrying tube that just begs to be touched.

As you can see from most of the projects here, it isn't necessary to construct the clothing and shoes and bags you want to embellish: dozens of companies create clothing "blanks" specifically for artists and craftspeople to work with, ranging from simple silk handkerchiefs to fully constructed garments. You needn't start out going to even that much effort, however: the perfect garment may well be hanging in your own closet, waiting for a new life. There's nothing quite as satisfying as taking a serviceable-but-boring shirt or jacket or pair of overalls and making it into something uniquely your own. You can embellish your stamping with whatever kind of sewing you like to do: embroidery or beading or appliqué. No matter what kind of clothes you wear or what kind of embellishing you like to do, the ideas on the pages in this chapter will have you looking at what's in your closet in a whole new way. On the following pages you'll find projects that will encourage you to alter everything, from your shoes to your old jeans.

TIPS

- Try this on an old jumper, dress, work shirt, or vest. Jeans and denim jackets are a lot of fun, but it's difficult to work inside the legs and arms, so you'll need to plan your work accordingly.

- You can transcribe actual entries from your journal onto these skirts, or you can just stamp whatever comes to mind while you're working on the garment.

- Photo transfers (see page 19) can be added. Try making transfers of photos or drawings from your journal and adding these to clothing.

- To make a skirt from your old jeans, you'll need to rip all the way up the inside seam, from the hem of one leg to the hem of the other. Then rip out the front seam to the bottom of the zipper or buttons, and rip out the back seam halfway up the height of the pockets. This is important to allow the front and back of the skirt to lie flat. Iron the seams all the way down, and then overlap the two sides under the zipper in the front and between the pockets, in the back. This is easiest if the jeans are laid out completely flat on a large surface. Stitch in place. Create the front and back panels out of the legs of other old jeans, or from any smooth, tightly woven cotton fabric of a weight similar to the denim.

ARTIST: *Ricë Freeman-Zachery*

iris-tattoo journal skirt

Denim has always been popular. Wearable art is gaining in popularity. Together, they're irresistible. With art stamps and quality paint designed for fabric, embroidery thread, and beads, you can turn a plain skirt into a work of art. Any smoothly woven cotton fabric will work, but it's even more fun to make one out of a pair of your favorite jeans; the more worn, the better. In fact, the embellishment will allow you to cover up any holes or stains, giving new life to a pair of old favorites!

1   Photocopy the iris pattern on page 134 four times, and then photocopy it four more times in reverse. Go over all the lines with a black fabric crayon, and then color in the leaves and petals. If your set of crayons doesn't have the right colors, you can use fabric dye sticks, which offer more variety. Just remember that they must be applied to the fabric, not the paper.

2   If the skirt is new, wash and dry it to remove any sizing. Place the colored images facedown around the bottom of the skirt, and iron on a cotton setting following the manufacturer's directions for using the crayons. Extend the stems and leaves as needed to reach the bottom of the skirt. If you want to add color with the dye sticks, apply them to the fabric and heat-set according to the manufacturer's directions.

3   Smooth the skirt out on a flat surface, and insert a piece of stiff cardboard or other smooth, sturdy material between the layers to provide a good surface for stamping.

4   Cut a small square of felt just a little larger than the "W" of your alphabet, and attach it to the plastic plate with double-sided tape. Apply ink to the felt, and allow it to soak in (you can work it in with the back of a plastic spoon). Use this stamp pad to ink the alphabet.

5   Stamp words around the flowers, improvising as needed to fill in blank areas.

6   Allow to dry for 48 hours and then heat-set.

7   Using embroidery floss, sew a simple stitch along all the outlines of the flowers and around the edges of any letters you want to emphasize. A split stitch makes a nice outline; others will add variety.

8   Add seed beads as desired to highlight the stamens of the flowers, various words or letters, and the pockets or other construction details of the skirt.

MATERIALS

- denim skirt
- embroidery floss
- seed beads
- screen printing ink
- fabric crayons and dye sticks
- alphabet stamp set
- iris pattern (see page 134)
- tracing paper
- plastic plate
- felt
- double-sided tape
- foam brush
- iron
- needles
- thread

collaged and stamped cigar box purse

You've probably seen these glamorous purses in boutiques for way more than you wanted to spend. They're cool and hip, they're a lot of fun to carry, and—yes—they are functional! Now you can make your own, and you're limited only by the cigar boxes you can beg, borrow, or buy. Because they come in a wide range of sizes and shapes, you can make tiny evening bags, big square totes, or anything in between. This stamped and collaged purse is lined with fabric and has little metal legs so it can stand up for display when it isn't being carried all around town.

MATERIALS

- wooden cigar box
- assorted decorative papers and ephemera
- stamps
- permanent stamp ink
- glass beads
- leather cord
- picture frame wire
- fabric for lining
- chipboard to fit bottom of cigar box
- small metal hinges
- upholstery tacks
- metal clasp for closure
- large split jump rings
- large decorative eye screws
- decorative "coins" or other pieces with a center hole
- small hooks clasps
- medium grit sandpaper
- collage glue
- glue brush
- water-based varnish
- small drill or Dremel tool
- pencil
- hammer
- needle-nosed pliers
- screwdriver (optional)
- metal snips (optional)

1   Remove the hinges and clasp from the cigar box, taking care not to split the wood. Sand the box inside and out, and wipe it off to remove sanding dust.

2   Collage the outside of both parts of the box with the papers and ephemera, using collage glue. Allow this to dry. Stamp over the collage using permanent ink.

3   When the glue and ink are completely dry, brush one coat of the water-based varnish on the box, one side at a time. Allow this to dry completely before proceeding.

4   Decide where the hinges will go, and mark the box with a pencil. Drill holes for the hinge screws. A Dremel tool works well. Attach the hinges.

5   Hammer four upholstery tacks into the bottom corners for "legs."

6   Drill holes for the closure. If you're using a standard clasp, use the screws that come with it. If you want to use a game piece and leather cord, drill the game piece and attach it with a screw. Drill a hole for the cord, and knot it inside the purse, pulling snugly around the game piece to check for length. *Note:* If the screws extend into the interior of the box, use either metal snips or the cut-off wheel on your Dremel tool to cut them flush with the surface.

7   Drill two holes in the top of the purse for the handle. Attach decorative screw eyes, centering them over decorative coins or other drilled pieces, if desired.

8   To make the handle, cut a length of picture frame wire 2" to 3" (5 to 7.5 cm) longer than the desired length. Thread on the beads, leaving 1" to 1½" (2.5 to 4 cm) at each end. Form a loop at each end, using needle-nosed pliers. Attach the split rings and small hooks, and hook the handle to the screw eyes on the purse.

9   For the lining, cut a piece of chipboard to fit the bottom of the cigar box. Cover one side with fabric, gluing the edges to the back side. Glue this covered board to the bottom of the box and allow to dry.

TIPS

- *You can collage and stamp on the inside of the lid if you choose. Often, though, the lids are interesting enough, and all you'll want to add are a couple of stamped images.*

- *Add charms, bells, beads, or other baubles to the purse, inside or outside. You can attach them with glue, or you can drill holes and attach them with small screws before you line the purse.*

- *Because the handle is attached with small hooks, you can make alternate handles out of other beads, braided leather, or chains. Almost anything that's sturdy enough to support the weight of the purse will work as a handle.*

ARTIST: *Anne Sagor*

silk shawl
Stamping on silk is easier than you would expect, and the results are spectacular—no one will believe it's been stamped! Silk blanks and plain silk garments ready for embellishment come in all styles and sizes, giving you lots of choices. This elegant shawl makes a perfect evening wrap, and the color palette you choose will allow you to make it as subtle or as bold as you wish.

1   Cover the work surface with either freezer paper or a white plastic tablecloth. Spread the shawl out on the work surface, right side up, making sure no fringe is tucked underneath.

2   Pour small puddles of fabric paint onto the Styrofoam tray. Dip the dry sponges into the paint, dabbing on a paper towel to remove the excess. When the sponge texture is visible, stamp onto the shawl, keeping the material as flat as possible. Repeat over the surface of the shawl, leaving some white areas.

3   Use a hair dryer to dry the paint.

4   Apply permanent pigment ink to the art stamps, and stamp on the fabric. If the shawl has to be moved during the process, make sure all the images have first been dried with the hair dryer.

5   Allow the ink and paint to cure for 24 to 48 hours, and then heat-set with an iron on the silk or cotton setting, placing a piece of tracing paper or sandwich paper over each area before ironing.

MATERIALS

- silk shawl
- sponges
- paints (we used Lumiere: bronze, olive, violet, and copper)
- ink (we used Brilliance Pigment Ink: coffee bean, Victorian violet, and copper)
- art stamps
- freezer paper or white plastic tablecloth
- Styrofoam tray
- paper towels
- craft sticks
- tracing paper
- iron
- hair dryer
- plastic bag

TIPS

- *To launder the shawl, use cool water and a mild shampoo or soap. Do not soak the shawl, and do not rub any of the areas that have been decorated. Rinse well, roll in an absorbent towel to dry, and then iron on the reverse side.*

- *Try dying the silk before painting and stamping it.*

- *Add small coordinating beads to the fringe.*

ARTIST: *Linda Woods*

stamped canvas shoes

Although these stamped shoes look purely decorative, they're designed so that you can stamp your shoes and wear them, too. You can choose colors and themes to coordinate with your other artwear, or you can create a pair of shoes that can stand—and walk—as works of art all by themselves. Hand-carved stamps work well on canvas, so you can carve stamps to make shoes for any special occasion, such as a trip or exciting adventure.

MATERIALS

- canvas shoes
- fabric paint
- art stamps
- sponge brushes
- ribbon (optional)
- spray sealer
- newspaper

1 Remove the laces from the shoes, and set them aside.

2 Crumple up newspaper, and stuff the shoes.

3 Base paint the shoes with fabric paint, and allow to dry.

4 Use the foam brush to apply the fabric paint to the stamps, and stamp the shoes. Allow to dry.

5 If your fabric paint requires heat-setting, put the shoes (without laces) in the dryer for 30 minutes.

6 When the shoes are dry, take them outdoors, and spray them with spray sealer. Use several light coats rather than one thick one.

7 Lace the shoes, perhaps using decorative ribbon.

TIPS

- *Add charms or buttons to the shoes, either by attaching them to the eyelets for the laces or gluing them on with appropriate glue.*

- *Paint or stamp the laces with colors or images to coordinate with the stamping on the shoes. Wide laces—either purchased or made from wide ribbon—will allow for a broader stamping area.*

- *Try stamping words on the shoes. You could stamp a very short story, a favorite quote, part of a letter, or a poem to create "Poem Shoes." Think of the shoes as three-dimensional canvases.*

stamped silk tie

This stunning tie is one that even the pickiest man would wear. It's elegant without being snooty, eye-catching without being flashy. We used Brilliance inks on charmeuse silk, which gives the fabric a subtle sheen. You can change the colors to fit the suit—it's the perfect wearable art for someone who can't get away with decorated denim at work.

1   Using direct-to-surface techniques, apply the ink pads directly to the tie. Dab the pads to get light colors, and press them firmly into the silk to get deeper colors. Pull and drag them across some parts, using all the colors except black.

2   Heat-set the inks with a hair dryer. The higher temperatures of a heat tool might harm the silk.

3   Color the back of the tie the same way, and pull the edges of the tie across several of the ink pads to make sure that the edges are colored. Heat-set with a hair dryer.

4   Ink a script stamp with the black ink pad, and stamp on the front of the tie.

5   Stamp leaves in copper. Heat-set as above. *Note:* Although the inks have been heat-set, do not wash the tie. Water will make the fabric warp.

MATERIALS

○ charmeuse silk tie

○ **ink pads** (we used Brilliance inks: pearlescent beige, graphite black, pearlescent jade, pearlescent lavender, and cosmic copper)

○ art stamps

○ hair dryer

TIPS

▪ *Make a matching tie tack by etching gingko leaves into a pieces of copper and attaching them to a tie tack blank (available at craft and jewelry supply stores). See page 21 for instructions on how to etch on metal.*

▪ *Stamp a domino or other game tile for a tie tack. See pages 60 and 61 for ideas and instructions.*

MATERIALS

- papier-mâché tube, 11½" tall × 3½" wide (29 cm × 9 cm)
- garment weight suede scraps: various colors
- two 1" (2.5 cm) brass hinges
- metallic cording
- 28-gauge gold wire
- 2 oz (57 grams) white polymer clay
- chalk pastels: colors to match suede scraps
- ceramic beads
- glass beads
- leather strap
- white tacky glue
- masking tape
- needle
- awl
- art stamps
- gold acrylic paint
- permanent black dye ink and refill
- black crafter's ink
- scissors
- toaster oven
- dust mask
- pasta machine or rolling pin
- pencil
- craft knife
- paintbrushes
- permanent black ink pen
- scrap paper
- sandpaper, 200 grit
- 18 kt. gold leafing pen
- small screwdriver (Phillips head)
- removable 2" × 4" (5 cm × 10 cm) white label stickers
- ruler
- graph paper
- leather punch

stamped suede carrying tube *This*

stamped suede carrying tube is a wonderful gift for any stamper—functional art that is truly a sensory delight to both the eyes and the fingers.

PREPARE THE TUBE

1   Measure 1½" (4 cm) in from the open end of the tube, and mark with a pencil. Put masking tape around the tube at the pencil mark to use as a cutting guide; cut around the tube with a craft knife. Remove the tape, and sand the cut edge.

2   Place the open end of the tube on the lid, and trace around it with a pencil. Cut out this circle, and sand the edges.

3   Use tacky glue to adhere the circle to the open end of the tube. Allow to dry for 30 minutes, and then apply more glue to the seam. Allow this to dry completely.

4   To make the door panel, measure 5" (12.5 cm) in from each end to find the middle of the tube, and mark it on the seamless side. Use label stickers to make a 3" × 4" (7.5 cm × 10 cm) cutting guide the door. Find the middle of both labels by folding them in half lengthwise, and then open them back up and align this fold mark with the center marks on the tube. Use the craft knife to cut out the door panel. Cut off an additional ⅛" (3 mm) from the door panel to allow for hinges. Sand all cut edges.

5   Paint the interior with the gold acrylic paint and set the tube aside to dry.

PREPARE THE CLAY DOOR

1   Condition the clay (see page 15). Run the clay through a pasta machine on setting #7, or roll it out with a rolling pin to about a ⅛" (3 mm) thickness.

2   Lay the clay over the papier-mâché door, and trim the clay to fit.

3   Arrange the hinges on the clay, and pierce through each hole in the hinges, making sure to reach the door panel. Remove the clay, and finish piercing through the door. Align the hinges on the tube; mark and pierce hinge holes. Pierce holes in the tube and the door for the bead closure and loop.

4   Use a craft knife to shave chalk pastels on the clay door panel, and rub the colors into the clay with your fingers. Buff with a tissue. Stamp with black crafter's ink.

5   Preheat the toaster oven to 275°F (135°C). Coat the outside of the door panel with glue, and lay the clay over it, matching up the holes for the hinges. Press the clay in place, being careful not to smear the stamped image. Bake for 15 to 20 minutes. Allow to cool.

6   Check the door to see if it fits in the tube properly. Sand if necessary.

7   Detail the edges of the door with the gold pen. When the edges are dry, paint the inside of the door with the gold acrylic paint.

COVER THE TUBE

1 Glue circles of unstamped suede to the two ends. Trim closely.

2 Cut the remaining suede into pieces, and stamp with the permanent black ink.

3 Begin covering the tube by applying pieces of suede at either end of the door opening, using a small paint brush to apply tacky glue to both the tube and the back of the suede. Cover the rest of the tube, cutting pieces to fit as you go along. Try triangles and circles, as long as all the pieces fit together snugly with no gaps.

ATTACH THE DOOR PANEL AND STRAP

1 Put the door in place, and attach the hinges.

2 Attach the bead and loop closure.

3 Pierce holes in the leather strap and the ends of the tube. Use wire to attach the strap, threading beads onto the wire as desired. Cover the ends of the wire, on the inside of the tube, with masking tape.

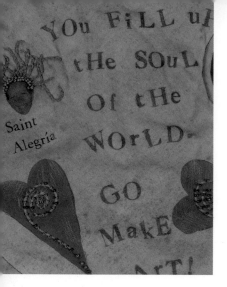

saint alegría shawl *Subtitled "Be Happy: Make Art,"* *this shawl is both wearable art and talismanic costume. It combines stamping with dyeing, beading, stenciling, embroidery, photo transfers, and painting. When you wear it, you can't help but smile and be inspired.*

MATERIALS

- 4 yards (366 cm) perma-press muslin, 48" (122 cm) wide
- 2 yards (183 cm) cream flannel, 48" (122 cm) wide
- 2 yards (183 cm) batting, 48" (122 cm) wide
- spray dye: magenta, purple, blue, and green
- fabric paints: magenta, purple, and blue-green
- spray bottle of water
- alphabet stamps in various sizes
- art stamps
- blank stencil-making material
- craft knife
- letter stencils
- iron-on photo transfer of your face
- various smaller iron-on transfers
- embroidery thread in coordinating colors
- beads (we used seed beads and bugle beads)
- beading thread
- needle
- pins
- sewing machine
- washer and dryer
- iron and ironing board

DYE THE FABRIC

1   Launder the muslin and the flannel. Cut the muslin into two 2-yard (183 cm) pieces. Set one aside.

2   Dampen the other piece of muslin, and hang it outside on a clothesline. Spray the dye onto the damp fabric. Mist the fabric with the water bottle as you go to make the dye run, and mix. Continue spraying until you're pleased with the colors. Allow to dry, and then tumble in a hot dryer for 30 minutes to heat-set, or follow the manufacturer's directions. Press if necessary.

3   Lay the dyed muslin on top of the other piece. Fold in half to find the middle; then cut at an angle in a scalloped pattern so that when the fabric is unfolded it will form a triangle. The scalloped edge can be cut freehand; or you can make a paper pattern.

4   Cut the flannel and the batting to match the shape of the muslin. Set the flannel aside.

DECORATE THE SHAWL

1   Iron a transfer of your face (see pages 19 and 20) on the muslin. Add other transfers as desired.

2   Using a fine-tip pen, draw designs on the transferred face. Appliqué a hat made from scrap material, if desired. Stamp the rest of the shawl with the alphabet stamps and other images. This shawl has hand-carved designs along the edges, made with stamps carved especially for it.

3   Trace your hands onto the blank stencil-making material, cut them out, and use the stencils to paint hands on your shawl. Use a small alphabet stamp set to put words inside the hand shapes. Let the paint dry, and then iron the shawl to heat-set the paint, or follow manufacturer's directions.

4   Make a sandwich of the muslin and batting: place the plain muslin on a flat surface with the batting on top of it and the decorated muslin on top of that, right side up. Pin together. Sew this sandwich together, using a basting stitch. It's easier to keep it smooth if you start from the middle, sewing around the face and then working out from that. Sew the edges together.

5   Embroider and embellish the shawl as desired Add beads, embroider the lines you drew on the transferred face, and do all detail work.

PUT THE SHAWL TOGETHER

1   Lay the flannel out flat, and lay the shawl sandwich on top of it, wrong side up.

2   Pin together carefully, making sure both pieces are smooth.

3   Sew together on the sewing machine, leaving an opening to turn the shawl. Turn the shawl and smooth it flat.

4   Pin all the way around the edge and then topstitch to hold the shape. Catch the opening (where you turned the shawl) as you topstitch. If desired, add some quilting lines.

TIPS

- *Make the lining out of flannel for warmth or you can use a more traditional lining fabric for a smoother drape.*

- *Add tassels to all three corners. You can make your own out of decorative fibers.*

- *Sew on a decorative closure, such as a frog or large button.*

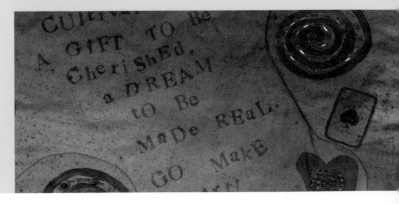

FOR THE
JEWEL BOX

Few things are more personal than the jewelry we wear. It tells the world something about us, whether it's a diamond ring announcing our engagement or a bolo tie announcing our cowboy status. As artists, our jewelry should reflect our creativity.

Almost as soon as we begin stamping, we want to make something more than cards and envelopes. Something more lasting, something more visible. Most of us have created pins and bracelets from shrink plastic or from stamped paper and card stock that we've laminated. Some of us have begun to make stamped jewelry from polymer clay. Now artists are combining stamping with glass and metal to make truly lasting pieces of wearable art.

No longer is the creation of beautiful, durable jewelry the province of only a select group of artisans. New materials, such as clay combined with precious metals, allow the home crafter to create metal jewelry that was previously within the reach of only those with access to a jewelry bench and metalworking tools. New techniques allow the rubber-stamp artist to etch stamp designs directly onto metal, creating permanent stamped metal pieces. No longer are these artists limited to delicate, ephemeral jewelry. We'll also explore innovative polymer-clay techniques that will allow you to easily create lightweight clay pieces that look nothing at all like simple clay—you'll be able to imitate metal and marble.

On the following pages, you'll find jewelry made of clay, wood, glass, leather, and metal, as well as pieces fashioned from stamped game tiles. And no matter what kind of art you like to create—from collage (see the soldered glass charms on pages 64 and 65) to beading (check out the beaded leather brooch on pages 66 and 67)—there's something here that will inspire you. With the guidance of the artists that have contributed to this book, rubber-stamp artists can begin to explore the art of personal adornment, in all its excitement and beauty.

wooden "play" brooch

Here's a brooch made from vintage bits and pieces that might normally be tossed—a child's block, a New Year's Eve rattle, old guitar parts. It's lots of fun to wear, and sure to evoke grins of recognition and memories of a favorite keepsake.

MATERIALS

- wooden toy building block
- vintage tin litho (check flea markets for tin rattles and tops, old metal signs, or cans)
- guitar pegs
- pin back
- vintage sheet music
- art stamps
- alphabet stamps
- permanent crafter's ink
- paint (we used and recommend Lumiere)
- brush
- tin snips
- drill with small bits in several sizes
- small brass screws or nails
- small screwdriver or hammer
- heat tool
- matte sealer

1   If the building block is not colored, paint it with several colors of paint. Allow to dry.

2   Use the tin snips to cut out the tin litho—pick a part of the metal that has appealing colors or figures.

3   Drill holes in the metal, and attach the metal to the block with small nails or screws.

4   Drill holes in the top and bottom edges of the block to attach old guitar pegs. Glue in place.

5   Use the alphabet stamps and the permanent ink to stamp "Play"" on the front of the block. Stamp music images on the back and edges, as desired. Heat-set all the stamped images, using the heat tool.

6   Cut out bits of vintage sheet music, and glue them to the guitar pegs. Allow to dry.

7   Apply matte sealer to the block. Allow to dry.

8   Use the small screws to attach the pin back.

TIPS

- *You can find vintage guitar parts in some music stores that repair instruments. Ask for old, usable parts; they are usually inexpensive.*

- *Check flea markets, estate sales, and garage sales for bits and pieces of old toys, office equipment, and other vintage pieces that can be cut apart and used on jewelry.*

- *Look through that box of old toys saved from your childhood; surely there's a block or a metal car or something else that would make a terrific piece of wearable art.*

TIPS

- *Drill holes in the dominos before stamping or painting to make them into charms or pendants or to hang beads from the dominos themselves.*

- *You can use the metallic paint pens to create a background before stamping: scribble several colors of Marvy Metallics on the surface of the domino, and then mist it with water from a fine spray bottle, tilting the domino to encourage the colors to mix. Allow to dry, then stamp, heat-set, and seal as usual.*

- *Attach dominos to larger glass chips to make pins. Sand the edges of the glass as necessary.*

ARTIST: *Anne Sagor*

domino bracelet *This bracelet is made from tiny dominos and decorated with even tinier ones, along with beads and charms and assorted dangles. Surprisingly, dominos provide an excellent surface for stamping; and in addition to bracelets, you can make all sorts of other jewelry, such as the earrings seen here.*

1 Lightly sand the back of the dominos. (You can stamp on the front side if you wish; the dots can complement the stamped design.) Wipe the domino to remove any sanding dust.

2 Paint the sides of each domino with the metallic paint pen, and allow them to dry completely.

3 Stamp the images on the dominos with the permanent black ink. Choose images that are slightly larger than the dominos so that the surface is completely covered. Heat-set the ink. For Memories ink, use a hair dryer; for Brilliance ink, use a heat tool.

4 Use the colored pencils to add color to lips, eyes, and cheeks.

5 Pour a small amount of sealer such as Diamond Glaze into a plate, and apply it to the stamped surface with a brush. Use the pin to pop any bubbles in the glaze. Allow the glaze to dry thoroughly. Apply a coat of glaze to the back and sides, and allow that to dry.

6 Stamp the glass chips, and heat-set the ink. Apply a coat of the matte adhesive to all sides of the glass chips, and allow to dry.

7 Glue the tiny dominos to the glass chips, and allow them to dry.

8 Using the gold wire and jump rings, attach the beads and charms to the bracelet blank, making sure that they all face the same way. Glue the dominos and the glass chips to the bracelet, and allow to dry.

MATERIALS

- dominos
- **bracelet blank** (squares or circles of metal linked by rings)
- **package of colored glass chips**
- sandpaper
- **paint pen** (we recommend Marvy Metallics)
- **black permanent stamping ink** (we recommend Memories black ink or Brilliance black ink)
- colored pencils
- **sealer** (we recommend Diamond Glaze)
- **matte sealer** (such as PPA Matte)
- plastic plate or palette
- brush
- straight pin
- **adhesive** (such as E6000 or jewelry glue)
- gold wire
- needle-nosed pliers
- gold jump rings
- charms
- beads

"thought girl" necklace

This gorgeous pendant has the look of an image painted on bone or old ivory, but it's created with polymer clay. The stamped clay is wrapped around a core of clay, making it substantial rather than lightweight. The frosted glass beads add to the vintage look.

MATERIALS

- polymer clay: white, black, and translucent (we recommend Premo)
- gold powder: sunset gold (we recommend Pearl Ex)
- art stamps
- heat-set pigment inks: eggplant, ochre (note: regular pigment inks won't work)
- beads
- cord
- small tassel
- automotive sandpaper in the following grits: 300, 450, 600, and 1000
- pasta machine (optional but very useful) or acrylic brayer
- oven thermometer (optional but, again, very useful)
- rubbing alcohol
- facial tissue
- long, thin awl
- craft knife
- scrap card stock
- thin skewer
- dental floss threaders
- super glue
- gel pen

TO MAKE THE BEAD

1   Condition $1/4$ of the package of white clay by running it 10 to 15 times through the pasta machine set on the thickest setting. If you don't have a pasta machine, condition the clay by working it with your hands, over and over, until it's soft.

2   Make a snake of the clay, about $3/4$" (18 mm) wide and $2 1/2$" (6.5 cm) long. Set it aside.

3   Put the rest of the conditioned white clay back through the pasta machine on the middle setting. Make a square that is at least $2 1/2$" (6.5 cm) square. If you don't have a pasta machine, use a brayer to flatten the clay.

4   Stamp the girl on this sheet, using the eggplant ink. Over-stamp this image with the mosaic stamp, using the ochre ink.

5   Clean your pasta machine's rollers with rubbing alcohol and a tissue. Condition a small amount of the translucent clay and run it through the pasta machine on the thinnest setting.

6   Lay the translucent sheet over the stamped sheet, starting at the bottom, being careful not to trap air between the two sheets. Your stamped image is now somewhat protected by the translucent sheet, but you still need to be careful not to smear the ink. Run this two-layered sheet through the pasta machine on a medium setting.

7   Take the snake you made in step 2 and cover it with the two-layered sheet. Trim the snake edges so that it fits.

8   Condition a small amount of black clay, and add a pinch of gold pigment powder. To mix the powder into the clay, add a bit to the middle of a piece of clay, and roll the clay into a ball. Roll the ball out into a snake, and bend the snake back into itself. Twist the snake, and roll it into a ball again. Repeat this several times, adding powder each time until you get the color you want. Run this clay through the pasta machine on a medium setting.

9   Cut two pieces of the black clay approximately the size of the ends of the bead, and place them on the top and bottom. Push down carefully to seal. Trim to fit, and rub the edges smooth.

10   Add another, smaller piece of black clay (without gold powder) to each end. Press carefully to join.

11   Using the awl, poke a hole down the center of the bead as far as the awl will reach, and then turn the bead around and poke the hole the rest of the way. Insert the

STRINGING THE BEAD

1 Cut the cording 2" to 3" (5 cm to 7.5 cm) longer than you want it to be.

2 Fold the cording in half to find the center.

3 Thread the cording on the floss threader, centering the threader in the middle, and pull the threader and cording through the bead. Cut the floss threader with scissors to remove it from the cording.

4 Add beads to the thread loop at the top of the tassel, using another floss threader.

5 Tie the tassel to the bottom of the cord with a knot. Pull the cord up to tighten the knot against the bottom of the bead. Apply super glue to the knot, and allow it to dry.

6 Add beads to the cord at the top of the bead, and knot the ends. Secure with a drop of super glue.

7 Use a gel pen to sign your name to the bottom of the bead.

bamboo skewer in the hole to widen it. The hole needs to be large enough to accommodate two thicknesses of your chosen cording. Finish each end with a silver bead pressed carefully into the black clay.

12 Accordion-fold the scrap card stock to make a nest for the bead during baking.

13 Bake according to the manufacturer's instructions. Allow the bead to cool completely.

14 Wet sand the bead with automotive sandpaper. Begin with 300 grit, then 450, then 600, and then 1000. It takes a while, but the results are worth it.

TIPS

- *Add charms or beads to the bottom of the clay bead, instead of a tassel, or create smaller clay beads in complementary colors.*

- *Instead of wrapping the stamped clay around a snake, you can leave it flat to create brooch or a piece to attach to a journal cover; be sure to apply a couple of coats of sealer to protect it.*

ARTIST: *Donna Goss*

soldered art charm jewelry These
soldered glass charms are a wonderful way to both showcase and protect your stamped artwork. You can either stamp miniature works of art, or you can create larger pieces and make tiny color copies to preserve under glass. You can create simple charms, like the brooch seen here; or you can add jump rings for beads and other charms as was done with the necklace.

1   Trim the artwork to the size of the glass. Plug in your soldering iron, and allow it to heat, if necessary.

2   Trim the mat board or illustration board to the size of the artwork and glass. Be sure the glass is clean on both sides. Make a sandwich of the mat board and glass, with the artwork in between.

3   Wrap the copper foil tape around the edges to hold everything together. Press firmly, and burnish with the bone folder.

4   Lay the sandwich on the old towel, glass side up. Brush liquid flux over the copper tape on this side.

5   Solder the fluxed edge by touching the tip of the soldering iron to the coil of solder as you run the tip down the length of copper tape. This requires some practice, but it's not too difficult, and the solder will stick only to the fluxed tape.

6   The charm will be hot, so turn it over using the needle-nosed pliers. Apply flux to the back, and solder it.

7   Place the charm in the vise to solder the edges. Solder one edge at a time, turning the charm so that the edge you're working on is on top.

8   Allow the charm to cool, and then clean the glass with alcohol on a cotton ball to remove any flux.

9   Glue the pin back to the mat board back, and allow it to dry.

MATERIALS
- artwork
- glass
- mat board or illustration board
- **solder** (unleaded, no flux)
- pin back
- **glue** (such as E6000 or Quick Grab)
- copper foil tape
- soldering iron
- vise
- liquid flux
- small paintbrush
- scissors
- needle-nosed pliers
- rubbing alcohol
- cotton ball
- glass cleaner
- bone folder
- old dish towel

TIPS

- *Solder jumps rings to the charm to make a necklace, or add beads, **milagros**, or other charms.*

- *Solder jump rings to the sides of a half dozen charms, and join them to make a bracelet.*

- *For jewelry with a visible back (such as pendants or earrings), use two pieces of glass, rather than a piece of glass and a piece of mat board. Use two copies of your artwork, and you'll have a charm with art on either side.*

"hot!" stamped & beaded brooch

Beads add pizzazz to everything, even stamping on wood. Yes, wood: that's what these brooches are made of, at least the part that's stamped. The backing is made of leather, and then there are all those glorious beads! But never fear—the beading isn't complicated at all, as the beads are strung and then couched to background fabric, resulting in beading that's even easy enough for beginners. Add some dangling beads or charms, and you have a brooch that's hotter than a summer day in Texas.

MATERIALS

- wood disk
- fabric stabilizer (we used Pellon) **or felt**
- beads
- leather
- pin back
- batting
- stamps
- permanent ink
- acrylic paint
- small brush
- glue
- scissors
- beading thread
- beading needle
- embroidery hoop
- gesso
- sandpaper

1   Sand if necessary and apply gesso to a small wooden disk from the craft store. Let it dry, and then sand it again and apply another coat of gesso. Sand a final time, smoothing the surface to be stamped.

2   Using permanent ink, stamp the image in the center of the disk. Allow to dry. Color the image with acrylics applied with the small brush. Allow to dry.

3   Securely glue the disk to a 6" (15 cm) square of stabilizer or felt. Allow it to dry, and then put it in an embroidery hoop.

4   Choose beads that are the same size as the thickness of the disk. String these beads on the thread, and then "couch" them around the wooden disk by securing the beaded thread to the stabilizer with small stitches. Succeeding rows can be the same size or graduated until the edge is made up of seed beads. Add beads until the desired circumference is reached. Turn the piece over and apply glue to the back to secure the threads. Allow to dry. Carefully cut the stabilizer close to the edge of the beading.

5   Sew on strings of beads for fringe, or add charms to the edge.

6   Cut a circle of thin batting slightly smaller than the diameter of the beadwork. Cut a circle of leather the exact diameter of the beadwork.

7   Punch holes in the leather for a pin back. Push the pin back through from the wrong side so that only the clasp shows, not the bar where you'd normally sew the pin back to the fabric. This bar is now on the wrong side of the leather. Add glue to secure it there.

8   Glue the circle of batting to the back of the beadwork, and glue the leather over that. Allow to dry.

9   Sew beads to the edge of the piece, making a border and catching both the beaded front and the leather backing to secure the piece.

- *"Edge-beading" is formed by stringing more beads onto a length of thread than there is room for, resulting in a scalloped pattern. For instance, string five beads onto your thread, and then take a stitch three bead-lengths from the last stitch. The beads won't have room to lie flat and will form the scalloped pattern shown here.*

- *Rather than using thread for the edge fringe, you can sew with fine wire to make an all-around fringe that will stand up; this would be terrific for the rays of a stamped sun or for the arms of an octopus.*

- *Wooden disks come in various sizes and shapes that will allow you to create almost any kind of brooch you can imagine—heart-shaped, flower-shaped, oval, or square.*

ARTISTS: *Linda and Opie O'Brien*

etched metal
goddess bracelet *Until*

recently, most stamping on metal surfaces required embossing your stamped image, sealing it, and hoping that it wouldn't wear off. Now artists have discovered that stamped images can be etched into the metal itself, creating stamping that will last as long as the metal. This goddess bracelet, both sturdy and lightweight, is a simple introduction to a technique for which you'll find dozens of applications.

1. Cut copper into desired shapes and sizes with the metal shears.

2. Drill a hole in each corner of each piece of copper except the two end pieces; on those, drill holes in two consecutive corners and in the middle on the opposite side to attach the closure. Use the file to smooth the edges, and then sand the metal in a circular motion, using the sandpaper.

3. Tape the back side of each piece of metal with the masking tape, pressing firmly and covering the entire back surface.

4. Using the black Memories ink, stamp the front sides of the copper pieces. Allow the ink to dry completely.

5. Wearing rubber gloves, pour some etching solution in the container. You need enough so that the metal pieces can lie flat, with no overlapping, and be covered by the solution. Use the tongs to place the metal in the solution and to remove it. For more information and safety precautions, see page 21.

6. When the metal has etched as deeply as you want it to, remove it from the solution with the tongs, and rinse it thoroughly under running water. This bracelet took eight hours to etch. Remove the tape from the backs of the metal pieces, and clean the backs with alcohol.

7. To age the etched surfaces, apply black, red, and green ink. Allow to dry, and then sand off most of the color. Apply matte sealer.

8. Attach the jump rings and closure using needle-nosed pliers.

MATERIALS

- 18-gauge copper
- tape (either clear or masking)
- jump rings
- closure for bracelet
- drill with $^1/_{16}$" (2 mm) drill bit
- metal shears for cutting
- metal file
- sandpaper
- alcohol
- PCB Etchant Solution (available at Radio Shack)
- art stamps
- Memories Ink (this is the only ink that will work for this process)
- plastic or glass container with a cover
- disposable rubber gloves
- tweezers or tongs
- needle-nosed pliers
- matte sealer

TIPS

- *Rather than using colored ink to age the metal, you can apply a patina (available in craft stores) or use liver of sulfur (available from Rio Grande; see Resources, pages 138 and 139).*

- *Set eyelets in the holes for the jump rings as in the "Mediate-Communicate-Advocate-Love" pendant on pages 130 and 131.*

pink bird necklace

The artist made this little pink bird using a technique called mokumé gané. *In this technique, beautiful patterns and colors are revealed as you slice slivers from stacked layers of polymer clay. Apply this multihued bird to a base of black clay to make a pendant, and hang it from a silk cord.*

MATERIALS

- polymer clay: white pearl, red, turquoise, gold, silver, copper
  (we recommend Premo)
- scrap clay
- art stamps
- turquoise heat-set pigment ink turquoise
  (regular pigment ink will not work for this project)
- cornstarch
- parchment paper
- large smooth tile
- pasta machine
  (optional but very useful)
- acrylic brayer (if you don't have a pasta machine)
- oven thermometer
  (optional but very useful)
- tissue blade
- toaster oven
- bamboo skewer
- thin round coffee stirrer stick
- jump ring
- needle-nosed pliers
- assorted beads and charms
- necklace cord
- gel pen

1   Condition clays by running them through the pasta machine one at a time, 10 to 15 times each, on the widest setting. Add white pearl clay to the red to make pink, and run it through the pasta machine. Add white pearl to the turquoise clay to lighten it, and run it through the pasta machine. Run each color of clay through the pasta machine on a medium to thin setting.

2   To create a mokumé gané block, stack the clay sheets in the following order: gold (on the bottom), silver, pink, copper, turquoise. Run this stack of colored clay through the pasta machine on the thickest setting, then on the next thickest, then the next thickest, working to progressively thinner settings.

3   Cut the stack in half with a tissue blade. Stack one half on top of the other, and run this new stack through the pasta machine. Your stack should now have 10 layers. Set it aside.

4   Make a mold from the bird stamp using the scrap clay. First condition the scrap clay, running it through the pasta machine on the thickest setting; then place the clay on parchment paper, dust cornstarch on the rubber part of the bird stamp, and press it into the scrap clay. Push firmly but not so hard that it goes all the way to the bottom. Remove stamp carefully, and trim and bake the mold, following manufacturer's directions for baking. Allow the mold to cool.

5   Dust the baked mold with cornstarch. Press your stack of colored clay into the mold, turquoise side down. Push down firmly so that all areas of the mold are filled with clay. Remove carefully.

6   Lay the clay face up on the tile. Carefully press the edges of the clay so that they stick to the tile. With the tissue blade, make a cut through the top of the clay, horizontally, from the top left corner to the bottom right corner. You'll be slicing through the bird image, cutting away the turquoise clay to allow the other colors to begin to show. Do this just a little at a time, making each slice very thin. Set each slice on the parchment paper and cut another. Keep cutting these thin horizontal layers until you are flush with the top of turquoise clay that surrounds the bird image. Be careful not to cut the turquoise itself. You will see some of the other layers peeking through the image of the bird that remains in the stack. Use the tissue blade to trim the edges of this remaining piece into a pleasing shape.

7 Condition the black clay, running it through the pasta machine on the thickest setting. Lay this piece on the parchment paper and stamp with the herringbone pattern in turquoise ink. You don't need to press down as hard as you did with the bird stamp; just press hard enough to get the pattern into the black clay.

8 Carefully lay the bird clay on top of the black clay, bird image up. Cover with a piece of parchment paper to protect them as you carefully push them together. Trim the black clay, leaving enough at the top to roll over the bamboo skewer. Make sure that this rolled-over piece touches itself so you'll have a channel for the necklace cord. Use the coffee stirrer stick to punch a hole in the bottom edge of the black clay. The jump ring and charm will attach here after baking.

9 Bake the piece according to manufacturer's instructions. Allow it to cool completely.

10 Cut the cording 2" to 3" (5 to 7.5 cm) longer than you want it to be. Thread the cord through the channel on the black background piece and knot.

11 Attach jump ring and beads or charms to the bottom. Sign your name to the back with the gel pen.

TIP

- *Use the scraps of the multicolored stack to create small beads or charms. Hang these from the bottom of the necklace, or use them in another project.*

TIPS

- *If the strip of square knots seems too daunting, you can fashion a closure with a simple knot, adding beads for decoration.*

- *Beads can be added up the length of the cord to the overhand knots. Choose small beads that don't overwhelm the stamped design.*

- *Choose waxed cord in colors to coordinate with whatever ink you use to stamp.*

tri~omino necklace

There are dominos, and then there are Tri-Ominos: three-sided game pieces with plain backs that are perfect for rubber stamping and embellishment. By preparing the surface to receive ink, you're able to create jewelry that's not only elegant but also lightweight and easy to wear. The intricate slipknot adds a finely detailed way for the wearer to adjust the length of the necklace.

1   Sand the back and sides of the Tri-Omino, and use your fingers or a bit of paper towel to smear the tan dye ink around the edges to age the game piece. Heat-set and allow to cool.

2   Stamp the image with the coffee-colored pigment; place the stamped side up on your work surface, and then press the game piece to it. Heat-set and allow to cool.

3   Color the sides of the game pieces with the copper pen, and allow to dry.

4   Use double-sided tape to attach the game piece to the wooden spool, making sure that the metal spinner on the numbered (unstamped) side fits into the hole of the spool. Paint a light coat of the glaze to the sides and top. Allow to dry. Wash the brush immediately in the container of water.

5   Glue a bead onto the top of the game piece, using the slick surface adhesive and following the directions exactly. Make sure that this bead has a hole large enough for the 1-mm cord. Allow the glue to cure overnight.

6   Cut the cord into a length between 36" (91.5 cm) and 42" (106.5 cm). Insert through the carrier bead that was glued to the game piece. Add beads on the cord next to the carrier bead as desired, tying knots to hold them in place.

7   About 10" (25.5 cm) away from the carrier bead, tie an overhand knot in each side of the cord. Decorate the cord ends with more beads, and knot the ends to keep the beads from sliding off.

8   To create the decorative sliding-knot closure, cut another piece of cord, about 10" (25.5 cm) long. Curve the two ends of the necklace cord inward, toward each other, with one end over the other. Tie the 10" (25.5 cm) piece over the two cord ends between the overhand knots on each side and the decorated ends. Then tie a series of 4 to 6 square knots securely around the cords.

9   Cut off the ends of the cord used to tie the square knots, and put a dot of glue on the strip of square knots where the cords were cut. The resulting strip of square knots will allow the wearer of the necklace to adjust the length of the cord by holding the strip of square knots and pulling on the ends of the cords. The overhand knots on the necklace cords prevent the necklace from being tightened too snugly.

MATERIALS

- Triangular game pieces
  (we used Pressman Deluxe Tri-Ominos; the regular version is not suitable for stamping)
- 1 mm waxed cotton cord
- bone and glass beads, assorted colors and sizes
- tan dye ink
  (we used Ancient Page Sienna)
- brown pigment ink
  (we used Brilliance Coffee Bean)
- copper metallic pen
  (we used Marvy Metallic Copper)
- glaze (we used Diamond Glaze for a brilliant finish)
- container of water
- wide, flat synthetic bristle brush
- art stamp
- slick surface adhesive
  (we used Aleene's Glass and Bead adhesive)
- paper towels
- heat gun
- wooden spool
- double-sided tape

found object talisman bracelet

This found object bracelet is an example of the artist's rich, complex jewelry. It's both symbolic—enhanced with special numbers and letters—and talismanic. Although it's made up primarily of found objects, you can add any bits and pieces of metal that you have and want to save: parts of old jewelry, pieces of a favorite brush (look closely to find the one included here), or a tiny key.

MATERIALS

- metal link bracelet
- copper wire
- silver wire
- jump rings (various sizes)
- metal shears or tin snips
- metal stamps
- art stamps
- permanent ink
- copper
- brass
- felt
- 2 shallow glass dishes
- fingernail polish (various colors)
- sandpaper (for metal)
- masking tape
- ferric chloride (or metal etching solution from Radio Shack)
- soap and water
- baking soda
- dish of resin
- screwdriver
- mallet or rubber hammer
- drill with metal bit
- needle-nosed pliers
- jeweler's saw
- small metal file
- variety of metal found objects (gears, keys, typewriter keys, washers, screws, lockets, snaps)
- other found objects (small glass vials, newsprint, images)
- beads
- buttons

1 Lay out all of the found objects, arranging them in a pleasing pattern the length of the bracelet. It's better to have too many than too few; you want a full, lush look.

2 Plan how you'll attach each piece. Some will need to be drilled with the metal bit, and some can be wired on. Others have natural holes through which you can thread wire or attach a jump ring.

3 Cut the copper and brass (or other metal) into various shapes and sizes with the metal shears. File the edges smooth with the metal file, and sand the surface with sandpaper. Use one of the techniques below to decorate the metal pieces.

4 To assemble the bracelet, lay these pieces at intervals along the bracelet, and attach them with jump rings or wire.

HAMMERING

1 Lay the sanded metal pieces on a stable surface.

2 Use metal stamps and a mallet or rubber hammer to stamp words, numbers, and letters into the surface. If you like, you can bring out the image by rubbing the stamped surface with permanent ink, allowing some to remain in the stamped areas and wiping the ink off the surface itself.

PIERCING

1 Stamp your selected images onto the metal using permanent ink. Allow this to dry.

2 Drill a tiny hole in the middle of the area that you want to cut out.

3 Loosen the blade of the jeweler's saw, and insert the blade into the drilled hole. Tighten the blade, and cut around the inside of the image. Loosen and remove the blade.

4 Use a small metal file to smooth the cut edges.

REPOUSSÉ

1 Stamp words or images or numbers with permanent ink. Allow the ink to dry.

2   Place the stamped metal, image side up, onto the surface of a dish of resin.

3   Use a small screwdriver or other similar tool and a hammer to hit the metal until the image is traced into the metal. When you remove the metal from the dish, the image will appear in relief on the opposite side. Keep this in mind if you choose words and numbers, rather than images: they'll be reversed.

ETCHING

1   Pour a little fingernail polish (or enamel paint) onto a small piece of felt in a shallow dish. This is your stamp pad. Stamp the images, words, or numbers onto the metal and allow them to dry. (*Note:* Kazmer recommends using a set of stamps for this process that you don't use for anything else, keeping them cleaned and oiled with beeswax when not in use.)

2   Cover the back side of these pieces with masking tape, making sure the whole surface is covered and pressing the tape firmly in place.

3   Pour enough of the ferric chloride (etching solution) into a shallow dish to cover the metal pieces. Place them in the dish, using tongs or long tweezers. Check them after two to three hours. If the metal is etched to your liking, remove the pieces. If not, leave them for another hour and check again.

4   When the metal is etched, removed it from the solution using tongs, and rinse well under running water. Scrub with soap and rinse again. Scrubbing the metal with baking soda will neutralize the corrosive. Rinse and dry the metal.

5   Sand lightly with fine-grit sandpaper.

FOR THE
HEART

As artists we want to share our work—to freely give our art to the people we care about. Often this is as easy as picking out something we've already created that we know will be perfect for someone's birthday, anniversary, or retirement party. At other times, we want to start from scratch, make a piece of art especially for the recipient. But what about those times when we're at a loss—when we need to make something for someone but haven't been visited by the muse of gift giving, or when we have a whole list of holiday gifts to create, and we know that every single person on it expects something made especially for them?

We're here to help. The projects in this chapter range from the simple to the complex, but all of them are wonderful pieces you'll be proud to share. Some are great all-purpose gifts—the cool yet practical beaded leather bookmarks are perfect for all sorts of people; almost everyone reads. The stamped and collaged envelopes and the book of good wishes will go through the mail to brighten the day of whoever's lucky enough to find one waiting in the mailbox. These, like the Formica key rings (which are also stamped and collaged) are universal gifts—good for both sexes and all ages, from your teenaged son to your grandmother. Sheets of faux postage are wonderful to give to other artists, especially if you use their favorite images or reproductions of their photographs.

For gifts that are a little more involved, you'll find a beaded clay bag, which sounds odd until you see it; and then you'll want one for yourself! And there's the "Fine Silver Fish Tales" book—truly a labor of love and truly an artist gift, made as it is from beautiful materials that artists love. And last is a stunning quilt—this is one of those things that starts out as a little lap quilt to give to your best friend and ends up as a huge, bed-sized piece because you have so much fun working on it. No matter which projects you choose to make, the artwork in this chapter will allow you to create something special for someone even more special—truly a gift from the heart.

ARTIST: *Dorothea Tortilla*

our lady of guadalupe stamped leather bookmark

Because most people read, bookmarks make great gifts. The problem is that they're usually not much of a gift all by themselves unless you buy one made of expensive materials such as sterling silver. This stamped and beaded leather bookmark is an exception, though. A work of art in miniature, it's a gift any reader will use over and over; and because the actual beading is done on a backing rather than on the leather itself, it's easier to create than you'd expect.

MATERIALS

- 2 oz cowhide
- fabric stabilizer (we used Pellon) or felt
- beads
- soft leather (pigskin, lamb, or deer) in a color that coordinates with the cowhide
- stamps
- permanent ink
- acrylic paint
- small brush
- sealer (we used Mod Podge and a brush)
- glue
- scissors
- beading needle
- beading thread
- embroidery hoop

1 Use the scissors to cut an oval from cowhide. You can use a template for this if you want a perfect oval.

2 Stamp the image with permanent ink, and allow to dry.

3 Paint the stamped image with acrylic paints, using the small brush.

4 Glue a ½" × 8½" (1.3 cm × 21.5 cm) strip of soft leather to the back of the oval, and then glue the oval to a 6" (15 cm) square of stabilizer or felt. Allow it to dry, and then put it in an embroidery hoop.

5 Thread the beading needle (size 10, 11, or 12 "sharp" needle, depending on the size of the beads), and bead around the edge of the oval.

6 Apply glue to the back of the stabilizer to secure the beading thread. Allow this to dry, and then cut the stabilizer close to the beading.

7 To make the backing, cut an oval from soft leather the size of the beaded piece. Glue the leather to the beading, and allow it to dry.

8 Edge bead the bookmark, catching both the stabilizer and the leather backing. For instructions on edge beading, see page 67.

TIPS

- *For a truly versatile gift, you can attach a pin back to the bookmark; then the bookmark can be worn when it isn't being used to mark pages in a book. Add a charm or bead to the end.*

- *If you're giving a special book, one you know the recipient will read over and over, stamp a bookmark that's made just for it: use a fork for a recipe book, an airplane for a book about traveling throughout Europe, or a baseball for a book about Babe Ruth. Coordinate the colors of the beads with those on the cover of the book.*

TIPS

- *Creating an envelope like this one is definitely not a case of "less is more." Here, more is more: add layers of paints, colored inks, colored pencil. Work at building up the background and blending the edges of colored areas into each other.*

- *Use the entire front of the envelope, letting parts of the images flow off the edges for a deeper, richer surface. It's nice to lay the envelope flap out flat so that you can decorate it, too. The back of the sealed envelope will hint at the art on the front.*

- *Try using stencils made from various objects: screen, netting, mesh. Apply ink through these with a stipple brush or sponge.*

- *Apply ink to other surfaces—such as bubble wrap or a piece of reptile skin—to make an unusual background stamp. (Ask science teachers to save skin shed from snakes or lizards.)*

"dance the night away" collaged & stamped envelope

Everyone loves to get mail, especially since the advent of e-mail, when all too often the only things delivered by the postman are bills, ads, and the occasional catalog. Way up there on the list of mail we love to get is personalized, hand-decorated mail, something someone created just for us. "Dance the Night Away" is the very best of personal mail, so gorgeous and richly embellished that the lucky recipient can frame and display it—if only you can bear to drop it in the mailbox!

1 Stamp an image on white paper and enlarge it on a photocopier. Inkjet copies won't work for this technique.

2 Take the photocopy, envelope, lacquer thinner, and an old soft cloth outdoors; position yourself so that the breeze is coming from behind you. (*Note:* Lacquer thinner is extremely hazardous, and you should not breathe the fumes. We strongly recommend using a ventilator; not a particle mask, because fumes become concentrated when you breathe through them. If you don't have one, set up a fan outdoors. Position it behind you so that it blows fumes away from you. Don't work with your face close to the surface, and don't try to make a lot of transfers in one sitting.)

3 Place the toner copy facedown on the envelope. Pour some lacquer thinner into a small puddle on the back of the toner copy, or saturate a piece of old, soft cloth with the lacquer thinner and apply this to the back of the copy. Rub over the back of the copy, being careful not to shift the paper. Make sure to saturate the copy and apply pressure. This technique produces varying results; more lacquer thinner will cause the toner to move around more, resulting in a wetter look. Leave the envelope outside until it's dry. Save the used toner copy.

4 Cut out the image from the copy. You can use both the cut-out image and the paper from which it was cut out as stencils.

5 After the envelope is dry, add acrylic paint here and there, using a makeup sponge. Make a stencil of the mask, and use that to paint in the mask on the face. Use the stamp of a peacock feather to create the hair, stamping in various colors and building up many layers of color and patterning. Finish with metallic ink to add wisps. Use other stamps to work on the background, building up layers of color and masking the face as needed. Use script stamps to add words, and use the alphabet to stamp the title.

6 When all the inks have dried, attach the sequins with contact cement.

7 Stamp the image on the colored paper, and cut out with the decorative scissors to create the faux postage. Attach the postage stamp with the glue stick, and cancel it with a cancellation stamp.

MATERIALS

- envelope
- black-and-white toner image
- iridescent sequins
- acrylic paint
- makeup sponge
- stamps
- stamp inks in various colors, including metallics
- lacquer thinner
- soft cloth
- scissors
- decorative-edged scissors
- colored pencils
- contact cement
- colored paper
- glue stick

faux postage

Faux postage has long been popular with rubber-stamp artists, who often create their own stamps to coordinate with the decorations on their envelopes and postcards. Sometimes it's hard to use the postage, though, because you don't want to send it away. This lovely matted sheet of perforated postage is the perfect way to keep and display a sheet of your stamps—make one sheet to send away and one to keep.

MATERIALS

- perforated postal sheet and matching template (we used a template from 100 proof press)
- cardstock
- French text
- art stamps
- pigment ink (we used Brilliance coffee bean, Victorian violet, and Mediterranean blue, and Colorbox parchment and sky blue)
- permanent ink (we used Ancient Page sienna)
- colored pencils
- stipple brushes
- self-adhesive notes
- glue stick
- scissors
- double-sided tape
- paper cutter

1 Stamp images inside each perforated rectangle with pigment ink. To do this, mask each square with the self-adhesive notes, laying them right up to the perforations. Allow images to dry completely before masking and stamping the next square. If ink soaks through the self-adhesive note, discard it and use another to prevent ink from transferring.

2 Place the plastic template over the sheet, and stipple the background with the parchment-colored ink. Use another stipple brush to add a touch of sienna ink at the corners. Do this for each rectangle, providing additional masking if needed. Allow to dry.

3 Stamp the number 3 in blue ink.

4 Mask the entire sheet of stamps and stipple the border, first with the parchment ink and then with the sienna.

5 Stamp French script with the coffee-colored ink.

6 Enhance the stamped images as desired with colored pencils. Use them to add contour to the hats.

7 Tear out part of a page from a discarded French textbook. Glue onto the border of the faux postage sheet, and trim as needed.

8 Use double-sided tape to attach the finished sheet to coordinating layers of card stock.

TIPS

- *Although these stamps cannot be used as real postage, they can be affixed to envelopes to coordinate with purchased stamps.*

- *Try stippling or sponging color onto the entire square before stamping solid images.*

- *Use a cancellation stamp to create authentic-looking vintage postage.*

- *Decorate the front of a folded card by using double-sided tape to attach a block of four faux postage stamps.*

- *Use a block to decorate the cover of a handmade book or journal.*

- *Make faux postage to commemorate a birthday or anniversary—this is especially fun if you carve someone's image and use it on their stamps.*

"transaction" beaded clay amulet bag

Here we have an old office stamp ("transaction") combined with polymer clay and right–angle beading to create an amulet bag that can be adapted to whatever size and shape you want. You can vary the size of the clay panels and the size of the beads, and you can add more embellishments to personalize your bag. What treasures you carry in it are up to you.

MATERIALS

- polymer clay
- metallic powder
- beads (we used a large tube of 8/0 metallic seed beads, eighty-four 11/0 gold/bronze seed beads, and eighty-four 15/0 bronze/gold seed beads, also known as "Charlottes")
- black beading thread
- thread wax
- rubber stamps
- pasta machine or rolling pin
- tissue blade
- bookbinding awl or large needle
- toaster oven
- spray acrylic sealer
- foam board

DIRECTIONS FOR MAKING CLAY PIECES

1 Condition the clay by rolling and shaping it in your hands. Run the clay through the pasta machine on a medium setting, or roll it out to an even thickness, approximately ⅛" (3 mm) with the rolling pin.

2 Cut two rectangles exactly the same size. Stamp the both pieces on one side only.

3 Use an awl or needle to punch sewing holes on three sides of each piece. The easiest way to do this is to lay the clay pieces on a piece of foam board with a ruler lying between them. Punch evenly spaced holes, approximately ⅛" (3 mm) apart. Do this without handling or bending the clay by piercing through the clay into the foam board. (*Note:* The spacing of the holes depends on the size of the beads you're using. Size 8/0 beads work perfectly with holes space ⅛" [3 mm] apart.)

4 Rub the metallic powder into the clay pieces, both front and back.

5 Bake in a toaster oven following the manufacturer's directions. Allow to cool completely.

DIRECTIONS FOR BEADING (*See diagrams on page 135.*)

1 Discard any beads with small holes, because many thread passes through each bead are required for beading.

2 Start with 4 beads on the thread, and tie them to form a circle.

3 Go through 1 bead near the knot, and add 3 more beads (B). Sew back through bead C to make a circle.

4 Then continue through the circle to bead D. Go through D, and add 3 beads, sewing through all the beads, including D, to make a circle.

5 Sew through bead E, and add only 2 beads (rather than 3). Complete the circle by sewing through F, then E again, and then out through the leading bead, G.

6 From now on, you'll add 3 or 2 beads as needed. Keep the tension adjusted as you finish each circle, because it is impossible to fix the tension once you begin a new circle. (*Note:* Beads align like small crosses. Look for these as you sew.)

7 Continue until you have a strip of beading long enough to go around three sides of the clay piece and up around your neck.

ATTATCHING THE BEADED STRIP TO THE POLYMER CLAY

1 Lay the clay pieces beside the beaded strip to determine where they will fit together. Find the bead that will match up with the top hole in the front piece. Go out of the side bead and through the hole in the clay, from the back of the front piece to its front.

2 Add a 11/0 bead and a 15/0 bead on the front side of the clay piece. Go back through the 11/0 bead and the clay hole. (The 15/0 bead acts as a stopper to hold the 11/0 bead on.) Enter the original bead on your strip from the opposite side you came out of.

3 Continue around the right-angle weave to the next hole in the front clay piece, and repeat steps 2 and 3. Continue all the way around the front clay piece. Repeat for the back clay piece.

TIPS

- *It's easier to make a small beaded strip first (one that is approximately twice the length of the height of the clay pieces) and attach the clay to this strip; then bead the rest of the strip to fit around your neck.*

- *A beaded strip that is wider than 2 rows of beads will be more flexible and will allow the sides of your amulet bag to bulge or indent, depending on what you carry in it.*

ARTIST: *Corey Heimke*

best wishes book

Many artists first began using rubber stamps to create cards and to decorate envelopes. Experiments with stamping on surfaces other than paper and cardstock—such as wood—and adding collage, charms, and ribbons can take those handmade cards to another level of artistic expression. This little book is a perfect card-cum-gift for a special birthday and can easily be adapted to anniversaries, holidays, promotions, or other special occasions.

1 Lightly sand the wood as needed.

2 Use acrylic paint to paint one side of each piece of wood. Paint the edges, as well, and allow to dry.

3 On the painted backs, stamp words and phrases related to the occasion. You could also stamp on colored paper, cut out the words, and glue them in place for a more colorful book.

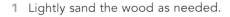

4 Create a collage on the front of each piece of wood. Use decorative paper, pages from discarded books, photocopies of photographs, and ephemera. Glue in place, and allow to dry.

5 Using permanent ink in colors to complement the collages, stamp images on top of the collages.

6 When the ink is dry, coat each stamped collage with a thin coat of the collage glue, and allow to dry completely.

7 Attach charms and three-dimensional embellishments with the tacky glue, applied sparingly with a toothpick. Be sure to place these only where they won't interfere with the closing of the book.

8 Arrange the tiles in book form with the cover on top to determine where to glue the ribbon; then use tacky glue to adhere it (you can attach ribbon temporarily with double-sided tape to determine exact placement).

MATERIALS

- wood rectangles
- sandpaper
- acrylic paint
- collage glue
- collage papers and images
- art stamps
- permanent ink
- brush
- tacky glue
- toothpick
- charms
- ribbon

TIP

- *If the alphabet you want to use is too large to allow you to stamp complete phrases on your pages, stamp the words on paper and then reduce the size using a photocopier; use colored paper.*

ARTIST: *Anne Sagor*

formica tile key chain

Artists can find inspiration in the most mundane things, and we're always on the lookout for items we can use for making art. If you've ever stood in the home improvement store fingering those samples of Formica and faux wood surfaces, knowing that they'd be perfect for something but not knowing exactly what, you're going to love what Anne Sagor has done with hers. These key chains can be personalized to make great gifts; you can make them into necklaces and brooches, too.

MATERIALS

- samples of Formica or faux wood
- key chain
- large jump ring
- sandpaper
- gold and silver washers or coins with center hole
- collage glue
  (matte medium or paper adhesive that can be used as an adhesive and as a sealer)
- art stamps
- ink
- gold leafing pen
- decorative paper and ephemera
- charms and beads and three-dimensional embellishments (optional)

1   Remove the label from the back of the Formica, and sand to remove any sticky residue. Sand the front and sides as needed.

2   Stamp images directly onto the tile or stamp on decorative paper, and then glue the paper to the tile. Do this on both sides, because both sides will be visible.

3   After the glue is dry, trim the edges of the paper as needed, and check to make sure that all edges and corners are securely glued. Trim the paper covering the hole in the tile. If necessary, add more glue to the edges.

4   After the glue has dried, use a gold leafing pen to decorate the edges.

5   Coat with a thin layer of collage glue, and allow to dry. Apply a thin coat to the back and sides, also. A second coat on the front and back will make the collage more durable.

6   Glue a washer or coin to each side of the tile, centering over the hole. Allow this to dry. Attach any three-dimensional embellishments you want to add.

7   Attach the key chain to the tile with the large jump ring.

TIP

- *You can drill holes along the bottom edge of the tile so that you can attach beads, charms, or other dangles.*

MATERIALS

- 20 grams Art Clay Silver regular clay
- 10 grams Art Clay Silver syringe with green tip
- 1¹/₂" to 2" (4 cm to 5 cm) fine silver wire (choose 12-gauge through 18-gauge for best results)
- black suede
- two 1" (2.5 cm) screw-tube connectors for books
- 2 pieces 5" × 7" (12.5 × 18 cm) wood for front and back covers
- 20 sheets of paper cut to 9³/₄" × 6⁷/₈" (24 cm × 18 cm) for pages
- 2 sheets decorative paper cut to 4⁷/₈" × 6⁷/₈" (13 cm × 18 cm) for end sheets
- 2 sheets papyrus cut to 4⁷/₈" × 6⁷/₈" (13 cm × 18 cm) (optional)
- 5" (12.5 cm) black binding tape
- fish rubber stamp
- saw or band saw
- bone folder
- marking pen
- ³/₁₆" (6 mm) paper punch
- neoprene rubber block
- plastic roller
- Teflon sheet
- two small strips of 1.2 mm cardboard (matte board or 3 to 4 playing cards taped together)
- craft knife
- leather rotary punch
- clamps
- drill with bit the same size as the screw-tube connectors
- paintbrush
- hair dryer, oven, or dehydrator
- small metal files
- stainless-steel brush
- sandpaper in grits 400, 600, 1200, and 2000
- butane microtorch
- firing block
- contact cement
- wood glue
- small brush for glue
- small kiln or access to a kiln

"*fine silver fish tales*" book

This terrific little book combines stamping with three of the materials artists love best: fine wood, handmade paper, and precious metal.

CREATING THE BOOK

1 From the suede, cut a fish tail to fit the front cover.

2 Use the saw to cut a 1" (2.5 cm) strip of wood from the front cover. You now have a 1" × 7" (2.5 cm × 18 cm) piece of wood and one that is 4" × 7" (10 cm × 18 cm).

3 Align the back cover and the 1" (2.5 cm) strip. Mark on the strip where the tail will fit.

4 Set the tail aside. Clamp together the two wood pieces, and drill two holes for the tube connectors.

5 Match the leather rotary punch to the size of the tube connectors, and punch holes in the tail to match those in the wood

6 Align the 1" (2.5 cm) strip with the 4" × 7" (10 cm × 18 cm) cover piece. Cut binding tape the length of the area to be covered by the tail. Press the tape in place and burnish it smooth. Glue the tail in place with wood glue, matching up the holes in the tail with those in the cover. Allow to dry.

DIRECTIONS FOR PAGES

1 Fold the page sheets in half and punch holes in those and the decorative sheets, aligning with the holes in the wood cover.

2 Crease all pages 1" (2.5 cm) from the spine edge, using the bone folder. This allows the pages to turn easily.

3 Assemble the pages and covers, using the tube connectors.

DIRECTIONS FOR THE SILVER FISH

1 Apply a small amount of olive oil to your hands, and roll the clay into a 3" (7.5 cm) tube. Place the tube on the Teflon sheet between the cardboard strips that allow you to roll the clay to an even thickness of 1.2 mm.

2 Apply a little olive oil to the rubber stamp, and stamp into the rolled-out clay. Press firmly, but not so firmly that the stamp goes all the way through the clay or leaves an impression on the back side. Cut out the fish shape with the craft knife. Leave the fish on the Teflon sheet, and dry thoroughly using the methods on page 17.

3 When the fish is completely dry, place it on the rubber block, and use the metal files to file any uneven areas. Lightly sand the top with 1200-grit sandpaper, taking care not to sand away the stamped image.

4   Place the fish in the kiln and fire it at 1600°F (871°C) for 10 minutes. Cool.

5   Brush the cooled fish vertically and horizontally with the stainless-steel brush, both front and back, to bring out the satin finish. Place the fish image-side up on the rubber block in water or under the faucet. Keep the fish wet as you sand the top and sides. Start with 400-grit sandpaper, then 600-, 1200-, and 2000-grit, in that order. Sand only the open, image-free areas on the front, creating a mirror shine and making the image of the fish more visible. Polish the top and sides. The back will not show.

DIRECTIONS FOR THE SCRIPT AND FISHING LINE

1   Write "Fish Tales" with the syringe clay on the Teflon sheet. Dry thoroughly.

2   Place the script on the firing block, and fire it for 2 minutes with the torch. Dip in water to cool. Brush lightly with a stainless-steel brush.

3   To create the dot for the "i," cut a small piece of wire and heat with the torch until it forms a tiny ball. Twist the remaining wire into an "s" shape for the fishing line.

4   Attach the fish, wire, and script to the cover with contact cement.

ARTIST: *Babette K. Cox*

raggedy stamped quilt *One of the many terrific things about this quilt is that you don't have to worry about having perfectly finished seams. On this quilt, all the edges are supposed to be ragged and frayed— the more, the better. The one shown here is lap-sized, but you can make yours any size you want. If you need to create several gifts, you can make small lap quilts. Or, for someone special, you can invest more time and make a bed-sized quilt, decorating and embellishing every square.*

MATERIALS

- cotton fabric (2½ to 3 times the yardage of your finished quilt in different colors; do not pre-wash)
- 100% cotton batting (cut to the size of your finished quilt)
- art stamps
- crafter's pigment ink
- images of faces
- computer with a scanner and printer (or access to one)
- transfer paper
- iron and ironing board
- sewing machine
- thread
- rotary cutter
- ruler
- cutting board
- scissors
- permanent fine-tipped black marker
- assorted yarns and fibers
- beads and charms
- walker foot for sewing machine (optional)

1 Plan how large you want your quilt to be, and plot the size on paper. You'll have finished squares in two sizes: 4½" (11.5 cm) squares and 9" (23 cm) squares. Four of the smaller squares will fit next to one of the larger ones. Cut pieces of scrap paper, and move them around to find a pleasing placement, and use those for determining how many squares of each size you'll need to cut.

2 To make the squares with the requisite seam allowances for fraying, cut the squares 5½" (14 cm) square and 10" (25.5 cm) square, using the ruler, rotary cutter, and cutting board. Each finished square will actually be two pieces of fabric, one for the front and one for the back.

3 Cut batting for each square; 3" (7.5 cm) for the smaller square and 7" (18 cm) for the larger square. Set the batting aside.

4 Make iron-on photo transfers from the face images, either enlarged stamped images or clip art. Cut out the transfers, and iron them onto the squares, following the directions on pages 19 and 20. Iron the transfers onto the squares.

5 Stamp on the fabric squares as desired. Heat-set.

6 Make sandwiches of the fabric and batting. Because the raw edges will be on the outside, you will not turn any of the fabric; make your squares with the batting sandwiched between the wrong sides of the front and back. Pin each sandwich together.

7 Lay the sandwiched squares out on a flat surface, and figure out where you want them to go. Stack two adjoining squares together, back to back (the decorated fronts will be facing out on each side). Pin them together.

8 On the sewing machine, sew together one side of the sandwich, sewing a ½" (1.2 cm) seam allowance through all four layers of fabric, right next to (but not catching) the batting.

9 Unfold the squares. You should have the seam edges all facing the front of the quilt. Continue pinning and sewing the rest of the squares in place. All of the seams will face the front, and the back will look finished, with regular-looking seams.

10 Some sort of decorative stitching is necessary on each square to hold the batting in place. You can stitch around the edges of the images, or you can stitch in swirls or other patterns, perhaps traditional quilting patterns. A simple "X" will do on some of the squares.

Fiɴishiɴg The Quilt

1 Topstitch ³/₄" (18 mm) from the edge of the quilt all the way around to seal the edges.

2 To make the raw edges fray, clip all the seam allowances right up to the seam. Make cuts approximately ¹/₂" to ³/₄" (12 mm to 18 mm) apart. Do this all over the quilt.

3 Heat-set the stamping by putting the quilt in a hot dryer for 15 to 20 minutes.

4 Launder the quilt several times. With each washing, the transfers become softer and the edges fray more.

5 Sew decorative fibers to the front of the quilt. Sew beads and charms to the quilt.

FOR THE
SOUL

Of all the aspects of daily life, we most often neglect the one that is vital to our existence as artists. We make time to eat, sleep, brush our teeth, and pay our bills, but how often do we set aside time to nurture our souls? We'll spend time taking a series of classes in oil and watercolor painting or we'll buy a set of expensive art brushes we need for our work, but we won't spend time or money to take care of that part that allows us to create our lives and our art. Whether we meditate or keep an art journal, go on retreats or take long, solitary walks, taking care of our souls is something we all need to do. And the art in this chapter will encourage you to do just that. Here you'll find funky art dolls, various inspiring shrines, an amulet bag just right for holding whatever amulets and talismans you need to keep near, a terrific die-cut book, and gorgeously stamped leather journal covers.

The process is as important as the product. Whereas the finished piece can serve as a reminder of your goals or a focus for your attention, the act of creating each one can be a meditation: on life, on art, on what's important to you.

Gather the materials you love most—your favorite rubber images, a stash of sparkly beads, a hank of colorful fibers, some scraps of supple leather. Think about what you want to make: a doll? a book? a shrine or bag? Shrines and amulet bags hold other treasures—things that inspire you, such as a snippet of an encouraging note, or a photograph you took on a trip. The art dolls can serve as a companion on your creative journey—you can make small ones to wear as pins stamped with words that remind you of what's important. And we couldn't forget journals—nothing nurtures the soul quite as thoroughly as a book where you can write and draw. We've included a blank die-cut book that can serve as an art or travel journal, a journal with its own house, and terrific stamped leather covers that you can make to fit the standard, spiral-bound art books that many of us use as everyday journals.

Whatever projects you choose to make, they're sure to satisfy your artistic soul.

house journal
*At its best, a journal is a house for the soul. It's where you keep the things that matter to you; it represents a the place you go to rest and recharge yourself—where you **really** live and play. This journal comes with its own house—a house for the house of the soul. The roof is removable; the journal can be constructed as an art piece or can be made functional with the addition of blank pages.*

MATERIALS

- wooden house box
- long strips of heavy paper or card stock
- acrylic paint: one light color and one dark color
- sandpaper
- wood primer
- crackle medium
- collage pieces
- decorative papers
- sheets of writing and/or drawing paper (optional)
- clip-art
- small found objects
- art stamps
- permanent ink for paper
- permanent ink for stamping on wood
- mat medium
- glue stick
- industrial-strength glue

DIRECTIONS FOR DECORATING THE HOUSE

1   Make or buy a wooden house box with a removable lid (see Resources, pages 138 and 139). Sand the wood smooth. Prime the house, and let it dry. Paint on a heavy coat of the darker acrylic paint, and let it dry.

2   Paint on the crackle medium following the manufacturer's directions, and let it dry.

3   Paint on a thin coat of the lighter acrylic paint, over the crackle medium, and let it dry.

4   Stamp the images with permanent ink on various papers. Let them dry (or heat-set, as necessary), and cut these out as desired. Gather all the collage pieces, and plan where you want them on the house, both inside and out. Cut these out, and arrange them the way you want them to go. Glue all the papers to the house using a glue stick or matte medium. Let this dry. Coat the entire house box with the matte medium, and allow to dry thoroughly.

5   Use the industrial-strength glue to attach the found objects to the house. Allow this to dry.

DIRECTIONS FOR MAKING THE JOURNAL

1   Measure the inside of your house box, and make a paper pattern about ¹/₄" (6 mm) smaller on each side. Use this pattern to determine how tall your journal will be. Cut the strips of card stock to this height.

2   Make light marks for the width of the house on one end of a strip of the card stock. Fold and crease. Continue to accordion fold, and crease the rest of the strip, making each panel the same size as the first.

3   Unfold the book, and mark and cut the top of each panel into a roof shape. If you want your accordion-fold book to be longer than the card stock you have, you can attach strips together with double-sided tape. Either leave a small tab to turn under and tape, or tape the end panel of one strip over the end panel of another, making sure the folds match up.

4   Decorate the journal with paint, inks, watercolor, collage, stamping, and any other embellishments you want. If you'd rather use the journal for writing or drawing, leave some of the pages blank, and insert sheets of blank paper, cutting them to the shape of the house and either stapling them in place or sewing them into the folds of the book. Make sure all glue is completely dry before putting the journal in the house and putting on the roof.

TIPS

- *Choose a theme for your house journal, such as "Creativity" or "Adventure."*

- *Make a travel journal. The box will help protect your journal while you're traveling and will make you think of "home" (what the word means to you, or how you feel about being away from home).*

- *Make a house journal as a house-warming gift for someone who's just bought a home. Add photographs of the whole process to the journal—from signing the contract to moving in.*

- *Drill holes in the edges of the roof of the house to hang beads or charms. Look for house-shaped* **milagros** *to ask for blessings of protection.*

ARTIST: *Babette K. Cox*

african man amulet bag *Amulet bags are*

perfect for carrying personal talismans. This one, complete with an doll inside, can hold small charms, baby teeth, perhaps a lock of hair. Write a blessing or wish on a scrap of paper and add it to the bag's contents. The leather cord is a perfect way to showcase your special beads.

MATERIALS

- suede
- copper tape
- wire
- polymer clay: black, silver
- art stamps
- fabric stamping ink
- twig
- assorted charms, beads, and bullion
- paper: coffee-dyed, black
- leather cord
  (in the same color as the suede)
- jump rings
- silver wax finish
  (we used Rub 'n Buff)
- waxed paper
- corn starch
- hot glue gun
- cyanoacrylate glue
  (for artificial fingernails)
- double-sided tape or
  rubber cement (we used
  Red Liner Wonder Tape)
- hole punch
- sewing machine
  (or leather needle and thread)
- pasta machine or brayer
- toaster oven
  (use for polymer clay only)
- timer
- oven thermometer
- heat gun

MAKING THE BAG

1   Sew two pieces of 3¹/₂" × 4" (9 cm × 10 cm), and sew them together on three sides, leaving a ¹/₈" (3 mm) seam allowance.

2   Stamp the leather with black fabric ink, and allow to dry, either by using a heat gun or letting it dry overnight.

3   Punch holes at the top two corners of the pouch and in the middle of the bottom. Attach gold jump rings. String beads and charms on the leather cord, and adjust the length. Tie the ends to the jump rings in the top corners, and secure the knots with glue. Attach the charm to the bottom jump ring.

4   Stamp "Ancient Mail" on a small piece of coffee-dyed paper, and glue the paper to a piece of black card stock. Apply copper tape to the edge of the card stock, and then attach the card stock to the bag with double-sided tape.

MAKING THE DOLL

1   Condition the polymer clay either by running it through a pasta machine about 20 times or by working it in your hands, rolling it into a ball and then into a snake, and then folding it back into a ball and working it over again. Do this until the clay is warm and pliable. Roll out a thick piece of black polymer clay. Cut a triangle that will fit into the bag and stamp it, using silver ink. Set it aside to dry.

2   Repeat with silver clay, forming a slightly smaller triangle. Stamp the silver clay with blue fabric ink. Allow to dry. Place the silver triangle on top of the black triangle. Cover with a small piece of waxed paper, and press slightly to make them stick together. Don't press so firmly that the stamping is blurred, however.

3   Push charms and embellishments into the body. After baking, you'll remove these and use glue to secure them in place.

4   Make the head. You can form one freehand, or you can use a mold or make a mold of your own from a bead: Dust the face bead with cornstarch and press into a piece of polymer clay. Carefully pull off the clay, and bake according to the package directions, about 20 minutes. After the mold has cooled, use it to create the face by

dusting the inside with cornstarch, and press a ball of conditioned black clay into the mold. Be careful not to use too big a ball, otherwise the back of the head will be too large.

5   Press the twig into the back of the head and remove—this will form a groove into which to glue the twig after baking.

6   Bake the face and body, following the package directions. Allow these to cool.

7   Rub silver wax finish onto the face.

8   Wrap gold wire around the twig, and attach a bead at each end. Using a hot glue gun, attach the head and body to the twig. If the head doesn't fit exactly, you can trim it using a craft knife with a sharp blade. Remove the charms and beads from the body, and attach them permanently with a dot of the cyanoacrylate glue.

TIPS

- *If you use snaps or hook-and-loop tape, you can make all the body parts removable and interchangeable. Make more than one face to express more than one mood.*

- *Sew decorative fibers onto the head for funky hair, or make hair out of colored wire.*

- *Before sewing the body closed, insert a wish or dream written on a tiny scrap of paper.*

- *Create a good-luck doll by attaching charms such as dice and four-leaf clovers all over the body.*

- *Make a healing doll—stuff her with herbs, or put a drop of aromatic oil on the fiberfill.*

funky fabric art doll

Every artist needs companions on the journey, and these are perfect: quiet, cooperative, inspiring, and adaptable. You can stamp their bodies with affirmations, ideas, or words of encouragement; and you can embellish them with all the beads, charms, and other bits and pieces you have left over from projects you want to remember. Make large ones to hang on the wall, and small ones to wear on your jacket. And, of course, they're wonderful gifts for other artists.

1 Stamp the doll pattern on the card stock and cut out each piece. Set these aside.

2 Cut the muslin into two parts, each big enough for all the doll parts with a generous margin around each. Spritz the muslin with water to dampen it, and brush paint onto the dampened fabric. Use three to five colors, and start with the lightest color. Leave some parts unpainted, and then paint more of those with each succeeding color. Spritz with more water as needed—you don't want the fabric to be saturated, but you do want it damp enough so that the colors will blend. Set the fabric aside to dry, or use a hair dryer to speed up the process.

3 Lay the card-stock pieces on the front of the painted muslin, and trace around each of them with the felt-tip marker. Leave plenty of space between the pieces so that you can cut them out and still have a generous margin for stitching. You can trim them more closely after sewing.

4 Use permanent ink to stamp images all over the painted pattern pieces before cutting them out. Let the images overlap, and go past the edges. You want a rich, dense look. Stamp a face. After all the stamped images are dry, lay this piece of muslin on top of the back piece, wrong sides together. Pin.

5 Use black thread to sew a running stitch, with stitches approximately $^1\!/\!_8$" (3 mm) long, around each body piece. Leave an opening for stuffing. Cut out each piece, leaving a margin.

6 Stuff each body part, inserting only a small amount of stuffing at a time and pushing it into place with the skewer. Stitch the body parts closed.

7 Attach the body parts. You can sew them with beads or sequins, or you can use eyelets, snaps, or washers.

8 Decorate the doll with beads, charms, watch parts, and fibers.

MATERIALS

- muslin
- fabric paint (we used Lumiere)
- acrylic paint
- card stock
- doll pattern stamp
- permanent ink
- black thread
- needle
- watch parts
- beads
- buttons
- charms
- sequins
- decorative fibers
- glue (we used Quick Grab)
- fabric markers
- brushes
- spray bottle of water
- freezer paper
- iron
- hair dryer
- felt-tip marker
- fiberfill stuffing
- skewer
- scissors
- eyelets and eyelet tool (optional)
- snaps (optional)
- washers and hole punch (optional)

"dream vision" diorama shrine

Every artist needs shrines—shrines to the muses, shrines for ideas we hope to capture, shrines to projects completed. These little box shrines are inspiring in themselves; you'll think of dozens of ways to add layers of meaning to capture the parts of your life you don't want to forget. A shrine to childhood—real or imagined, yours or someone else's—is the perfect way to save those gumball toys and baby teeth.

MATERIALS

- box with lid
- collage pieces, ephemera, photographs, clip art, decorative paper
- sting for hanger
- foam board or foam tape
- smooth card stock
- scrap cardboard
- craft knife
- cutting mat
- pencil
- permanent black pen (or pen that will mark on acetate)
- glue stick
- double-sided tape
- acetate
- art stamps
- ink pads
- sponge

1   You can either use a found box or make one yourself. Remove the lid, and set aside. Punch two holes in the bottom of the box (now the back of the shrine), and insert the string or ribbon for hanging, knotting it on the inside.

2   Decorate the inside of the shine, either by covering it with decorative paper or by collaging.

3   Stamp the images on the card stock, and cut them out. Mount the cut-out images on cardboard to make them more stable. Attach small pieces of foam board, cut with the craft knife, to the back of the pieces. You can also use foam tape. Use more than one thickness for some of the images so that the depth will vary. Use layers of foam board or foam tape to attach other collage pieces and three-dimensional objects.

4   To make the front of the shrine, first place the lid face down on a cutting mat and trim away the inside to $1/2$" (1.2 cm) on all four sides.

5   Make a decorative top for the lid by placing the it facedown on card stock and drawing around the outside and the cut-out inside with a pencil. Make the outside tracing very light, as it's just to give you an idea of the dimensions. Sponge color over the decorative lid top. Stamp and color images, and add collage elements, if desired.

6   Cut away the inside part of the decorated lid and fit it over the original lid. Trim the lids as necessary and then separate them.

7   Before you cut out the acetate for the shrine window, you can add a window image to it, either by stamping or by running the acetate through a printer (to print a scanned image) or a photocopier (to copy a clip-art image).

8   Trace the outside of the original lid on the acetate, and cut just inside this line.

9   Insert the acetate window between the original lid and the decorated lid, sealing them together with double-sided tape.

TiPS

- *See the Resources section, pages 138 and 139, for a kit that will let you make your own boxes in the size you need.*

- *You can use fine monofilament to dangle objects from the top of the shrine. Sandwich two stamped, cut-out images with the end of the monofilament between them, or use a tiny bit of instant glue to attach the monofilament to tiny toys or crystals or miniature game pieces, such as tiny dice.*

- *Use color copies of photographs on some of the foam board mounts. Stamp over the photocopies to achieve a layered image.*

- *Use monofilament to hang beads or charms or other embellishments from the bottom of the shrine. They'll dangle when the shrine is hung on the wall.*

- *You can also use these diorama shrines in constructing altered books. Cut out enough pages in the book to accommodate the size of the box. Decorate the front of the book to hint at its contents.*

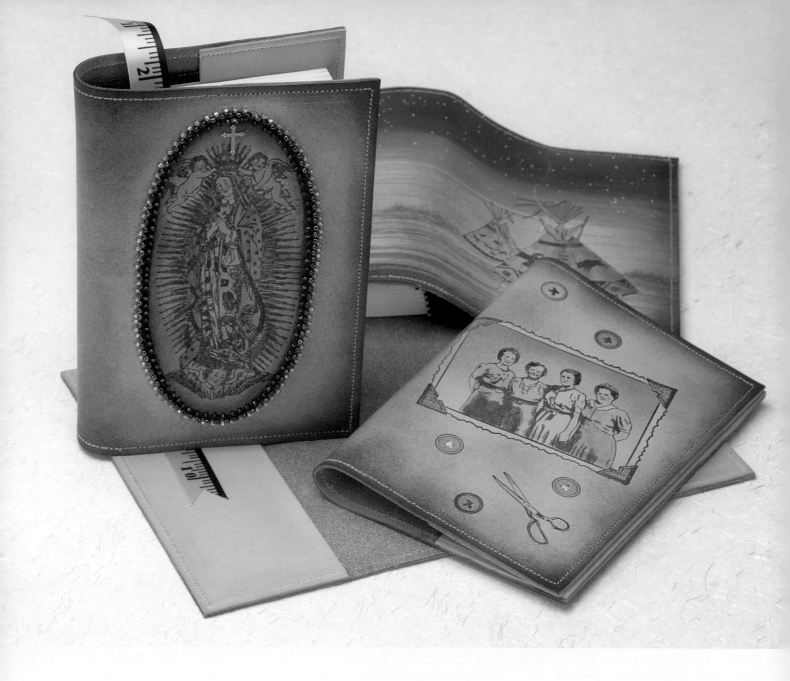

TIPS

- *These covers can be constructed to fit any size blank journal. For a 6" × 9" (15 cm × 23 cm) journal, the large piece of leather should be 10" × 14" (25.5 cm × 35.5 cm) and the two smaller pieces 2½" × 10" (6.5 cm × 25.5 cm).*

- *You can decorate the cover with charms or beads; punch holes in the leather and attach them with strong thread or long eyelets.*

- *Use metal stamps to hammer the title of your journal on a piece of metal. Drill holes in the metal, and attach it to the leather cover with eyelets.*

ARTIST: *Dorothea Tortilla*

stamped leather journal covers

There are almost as many kinds of journals as there are people who keep them, from inexpensive spiral notebooks that cost less than a dollar to elegant handbound leather volumes with handmade paper pages. If you love the look and feel of a leather cover but don't want to splurge on a new one every few months, the solution is at hand: a removable, stamped leather journal cover, designed to fit standard blank journals. Once you've made the perfect cover for your journal, you can use it over and over, sliding it easily over the existing cover of each new volume.

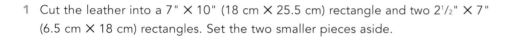

1   Cut the leather into a 7" × 10" (18 cm × 25.5 cm) rectangle and two 2½" × 7" (6.5 cm × 18 cm) rectangles. Set the two smaller pieces aside.

2   On the right side of the larger piece, stamp the images in permanent ink. Allow these to dry.

3   Use the paints to color all the stamped images. Make sure that whatever paint you've chosen is compatible with leather. Allow this to dry thoroughly.

4   Use the sponge to apply brown and sienna permanent ink to age the leather. Allow this to dry.

5   Turn the leather to the wrong side, and use a thin line of glue to attach the two sleeves to the short ends. This will form the pockets where the cover of the blank journal will fit.

6   Sew around the three edges of each sleeve. You can do this on a sewing machine, using a leather needle, or you can punch holes and sew by hand.

7   Use the awl to pierce the holes of the stamped buttons. Sew them with colored thread, and tie knots on the inside of the cover, securing with a tiny dot of glue.

8   Finish the journal cover with a light rubbing of furniture wax. Insert the covers of the blank journal into the sleeves

MATERIALS

- untreated, 3-oz, vegetable-tanned cowhide
- blank sketchbook 4" × 6" (10 cm × 15 cm)
- stamps
- permanent dye stamp ink
- fabric paints or leather paints
- sponge
- scissors or craft knife
- glue
- sewing machine or awl, needle, and strong thread
- colored thread
- furniture wax
- soft cloth

ARTIST: *Anne Sagor*

matchbox shrine doll *This project is both a shrine and a doll—the doll's body opens up to reveal whatever talismans or photos or mementos you want to enclose. The example here honors Frida Kahlo, but you can choose another artist, family member, or yourself: make a shrine to your artistic muse, with your own face on the doll and emblems of your art making inside the little box.*

MATERIALS

- matchbox
- lid of a cardboard or wooden box
- photograph or color copy
- jump rings
- seed beads
- alphabet beads
- decorative papers and ephemera
- craft knife with #11 blade
- acrylic paint
- brush
- glue
- card stock: white and colored
- art stamps
- stamping ink
- bead
- 20-gauge wire
- needle-nosed pliers
- awl or large needle
- colored pencils
- paper doily

1   Remove the cover from the matchbox. Insert the blade of the craft knife into the overlap where the cover was glued together, and cut through the adhesive to open the cover. Lay it flat. Glue decorative paper (we used black mulberry paper) to the outside of the cover.

2   Paint the drawer of the matchbox with black acrylic paint, and set it aside to dry.

3   Stamp the arms and head on card stock, and color with pencils. Cut out the arms and glue them to the outside back of the cover of the matchbox. When cutting out the head, make sure to leave a neck, or tab, to attach the head and allow it to be seen above the box.

4   Stamp the fan blade six times on card stock. Color them and cut them out. Glue three blades together for the front of the skirt, and glue the center blade to the matchbox cover.

5   Glue a piece paper doily to the bottom of the blades for a petticoat, and then glue the other three blades behind the doily to cover the back side. Make sure the front of these faces out or to the back.

6   To make the drawer pull, cut a piece of wire approximately 8" (20.5 cm) long. Glue the large bead to the end of the box, and punch a hole on either side of it. Insert the wire from the inside of the box out through the holes and then through the holes in the bead, so that the ends of the wire cross inside the bead and come out the opposite side. Coil the ends of the wire for decoration.

7   Decorate the inside of the box with paper, a photograph, beads, alphabet beads, charms, or other ephemera or keepsakes.

8   Use strong glue to adhere the cover of the matchbox back together, leaving a bit more of an opening than it had originally so that the drawer will slide easily.

9   Decorate the outside of the matchbox. Use large jump rings for bracelets.

10   Paint the lid of a cardboard of wooden box. Allow it to dry, and then layer colored card stock inside. Glue the shrine inside the lid and attach a picture hanger on the back.

TIPS

- *If the drawer is difficult to open, rub the sides of the drawer with waxed paper.*
- *Create a shrine for the whole doll to fit into by decorating a box lid and attaching her to the inside with ribbon. You could also hang her from the ceiling using monofilament (thin fishing line). Attach beads, charms, tiny bells, or prisms to the bottom of her skirt.*

hand book of art
Die-cutting allows you to create books in wonderful shapes. The hand book (or handbook!) shown here uses two dies: the hand and a key. By cutting the shapes from different colored papers and card stocks, you create a multilayered, richly textured book that can be used for recording your artistic inspirations.

MATERIALS

- die-cut hands: 2 each from black illustration board and gold card stock; 4 from parchment card stock
- die-cut keys: 3 from parchment card stock
- 24-gauge black wire
- cutting mat
- wooden skewer
- wire cutters
- glue stick
- hole punch
- Japanese screw punch or awl
- art stamps
- ink pads
- binder clips
- optional: small tags, tiny envelopes, eyelets, grommets, tooling foil and metal alphabet stamps, decorative-edge scissors, decorative fibers, charms, game pieces, photographs

DECORATING

1   Stack the hands in the following order: 1 gold on the bottom, 1 black, 4 parchment, 1 black, 1 gold. The black hands will be glued to the gold hands, so you'll decorate only one side of each. Put a pencil mark on the sides that will be glued together so that you'll know which to leave plain. Separate the hands, and decorate them with the stamps and inks, using copper and beige and sepia to age the pages as desired.

2   Punch holes in some of the fingers. Set eyelets in these holes to reinforce them so that you can later attach charms, keys, or other embellishments.

BINDING

1   Use the glue stick to attach the gold hands to the black hands for the front and back covers. Press firmly to secure, and trim as necessary.

2   Mark seven holes in the wrist of the front gold cover, approximately $^1/_8$" to $^1/_4$" (3 mm to 6 mm) from the edge. Punch the holes with the Japanese screw punch or awl.

3   Lay the punched cover on top of one of the parchment pages. Line them up exactly and use the pencil to mark through the punched holes onto the page. Stack all parchment pages together, with the marked page on top, and punch through them all. For the back cover, mark and punch as you did for the pages, using the front cover as a guide. Stack both covers and all of the pages in order, and secure them with binder clips.

4   Cut a 12" to 15" (30.5 cm to 38 cm) length of wire, using the wire cutters. Insert the wire from back to front in the bottom hole, leaving a tail approximately 1" (2.5 cm) on the back side of the book.

5   Thread three beads onto the wire, and lay the skewer along the length of the book's spine.

6   Wrap the wire over the skewer, and then thread it back through the same hole. You may have to wriggle the wire a little, but it will go through. Pull it snugly against the skewer. Repeat this for the other holes, keeping the wire snug. On the last hole,

thread on three beads, wrap the wire around the skewer, and go through the top hole. Then, without adding any more beads, wrap the wire around the skewer, and go through the same hole again.

7 Cut the wire, again leaving a 1" (2.5 cm) tail. Carefully remove the skewer by sliding it along the spine.

8 Wrap both tails of wire around the nearest loop. Wrap them a couple of times to secure them, and then cut off any remaining wire. Attach a charm (like the dragonfly shown here) to the bottom two loops.

FOR THE

FAMILY

If you're anything like me, you have photographs everywhere. There are some on the refrigerator and some on the bulletin board in the studio. There are some in old albums and some in my journal. Then there are all of those in boxes and drawers—good photographs I want to save but for which I've never found a home. Never mind that there's no time to organize them all; it would be wonderful just to have them somewhere so that they could be enjoyed and appreciated.

The photographs that mean the most to us are usually those taken years ago when we were children or even before we were born. These are the ones that we most need to look at, to keep in touch with our past and what it means in our lives.

In this chapter, we'll show you some marvelous ways to use those old photographs—and drawings, too, if you have them. You can use actual photographs, or you can make color copies. Even better, you can have your photographs made into rubber stamps, which opens up a whole new realm of possibilities. We'll show you unique ways to display your family's photos, such as individual albums and booklets or a shrine that will house not only the image itself but all the associated memorabilia, from newspaper clippings to old coins.

If displaying the photographs isn't enough, we'll show you several ways to make wearable art with family images—both on fabric and on metal. We have three projects that work together to create a carved stamp that's set into the cover of a handmade book, the spine of which is beaded and decorated with shrink-plastic beads—all wrapped into one book that's perfect for photographs or journal writing. And don't think that's all: there are even mailable note card magnets, which is a terrific, threefold project—a way to use family photographs, note cards that will bring a smile to the face of everyone who receives one, and a functional magnet that will last for years. Surprise someone in your family with a work of art designed by someone in ours.

"little ricë" photo transfer pin

Too often we keep all our favorite photographs hidden away in boxes or albums, where we see them only rarely. Using family photographs to make jewelry and ornaments brings them out in the open, where we can enjoy and share them with others. Once you discover how easy it is to combine iron-on transfers and rubber stamps, you'll think of dozens of ways to use the photographs waiting in those albums. This is one of my favorite photos of myself as a little girl.

MATERIALS

- **tea-dyed muslin** (see pages 17 and 18)
- **photo transfer** (see pages 19 and 20)
- matte board
- quilt batting
- leather scraps
- seed beads
- jump rings
- typewriter key
- *milagros* or charms
- pin back
- felt
- ribbon
- colored pencil or fabric marker
- manual typewriter or rubber-stamp alphabet
- art stamps
- permanent dye ink
- glue
- jewelry pliers

1. Iron transfer the to muslin, and then replace paper backing to use as a mask. Using permanent dye ink, stamp images so that they appear to be behind the photo. Add a light tint of color with the colored pencils if desired. Pencils can also be used to tint the ribbon to match.

2. Insert stamped muslin into manual typewriter, and type random letters. Alternately, this can be done with a tiny rubber-stamp alphabet.

3. Cut matte board to size, approximately 2½" × 3" (6.5 cm × 7.5 cm). Lightly glue thin quilt batting to the front, and then center muslin on this, wrapping the edges to the back and securing with thick white glue. Allow to dry.

4. Wrap thin ribbon around one corner, and glue to the back. Then cut small pieces of thin leather for each corner, wrapping them to the back and gluing in place. Allow to dry.

5. Sew seed beads as desired.

6. Attach typewriter key with permanent glue, and allow to dry.

7. Cut felt slightly smaller than the pin, and sew on the pin back. Glue the felt to the back of the pin.

8. Attach jump rings to milagros or charms, and sew to the bottom of the pin.

TIPS

- *Choose rubber stamps that reflect the interests or history of the person in the photograph.*

- *A hanging loop instead of a pin back can be sewn on so that the pin becomes a pendant or an ornament.*

- *Add wings, a halo, or a crown.*

- *Attach wires and beads around the edges.*

- *Stamp, type, or transfer words to add a message to the pin.*

As long as
we have
Art,
today is
beautiful.

DREAM

ARTIST: *Nanette Alexander*

"dream" booklet

This softcover pamphlet can enclose a special document, like a birth certificate or passport, or it might hold a handmade card for a birthday or graduation. What makes it special is the use of stamping combined with collage elements to evoke the mood of a treasured family photograph. Using a good-quality color copy will allow you to create more than one collage from your photograph.

1 Sponge the card stock with dye ink, masking and using a darker color to create three squares at the bottom.

2 Stamp the letters on card stock, and cut them out.

3 Color the edges of each cut-out letter with the gold leafing pen.

4 Create the collage with the color copies, found papers, pages from discarded books, photocopied letters, and other ephemera. When you have everything arranged the way you want it, glue the pieces in place, and allow them to dry.

5 Punch holes in the spine and in several folded sheets of paper. Insert the pages into the cover, and thread thin ribbon, embroidery thread, or decorative fiber through the holes to secure.

MATERIALS

○ color copy of photograph
○ white card stock
○ paper for pages
○ ribbon or fiber
○ dye ink pads
○ makeup sponge
○ art stamps
○ found papers
○ gold leafing pen
○ glue

TIPS

- *For a hardbound book you can create the collage on heavy, good-quality paper and then glue it to the cover of the book—either one you've purchased or one you've made yourself.*

- *You can do the same with boxes—once you've created your family collage, you can decoupage it to any smooth flat surface. Seal it with an appropriate sealer.*

- *Create a wearable version by making an iron-on transfer of the finished collage.*

"*charming one*" shrine

This breathtaking shrine is the perfect way to honor an ancestor, and use bits and pieces of braid or trim that might have fallen off heirloom dresses or uniforms. The artist used an actual photograph here, but you can work with good-quality copies if you don't have duplicates of family photos.

MATERIALS

- shadow box with matte
  (purchased at the crafts store)
- tin *nicho* (small shrine)
- old family photograph
- foreign newspapers
  (these are from Mexico)
- vintage book cover
- small metal stencil
- small brads
- various antique trims,
  braids, and fibers
- wire mesh
- small piece of old scrap
  metal
- old office stamps
- art stamps
- hand-carved stamps
- permanent black ink
- acrylic paints: assorted
  colors, including bronze
- gel medium
- small awl
- metal snips or old
  scissors
- wire
- thick white glue
- adhesive caulk

1   Paint the shadow box with acrylic paints, building up layers of color.

2   If the shadow box didn't come with a matte, create one from a piece of matte board.

3   Glue old newspaper to the matte, using the gel medium, and allow it to dry. Using the acrylic paint, stamp layers of images on the matte, over the old newspaper. Hand-carved stamps were used, but you can use any stamps that create a rich, layered look. Set this aside and allow it to dry.

4   Glue old newspaper to the back of the shadow box. Allow it to dry. Stamp over the newspaper.

5   Glue the book cover to the back of the shadow box, using the adhesive caulk. Allow this to dry.

6   With the awl, punch two holes through the book cover and the back of the shadow box where you want to the *nicho* to fit. Attach the nicho with wire, twisting the ends on the back. Glue pieces of the newspaper to the inside of the *nicho*. Allow to dry thoroughly. Stamp over the newspaper.

7   Cut out the face of the person in the photograph. If you're using a color copy made on paper, glue the paper to card stock before cutting it out. This will give the photocopy enough body so that it will stand up. Stamp over the body of the photograph, using old office stamps or numbers and permanent black ink.

8   Use the metal snips to cut a crown from the piece of scrap metal and to cut wings from the metal mesh. Punch holes in the crown and wings, and attach them to the photograph with small brads.

9   Attach the photograph to the bottom of the tin *nicho*, using adhesive caulk. You can create a cardboard brace behind it if necessary. Use adhesive caulk to attach the metal stencil to the top of the *nicho*.

10 Use white glue to attach the antique trims, braid, and fibers around the photograph, the *nicho*, and the matte. Attach wire to the back for hanging.

TIPS

- *If you don't have any old (or old-looking) trim or braid, you can age what you have by tea-dying it (see pages 17 and 18).*

- *If you don't have old family photographs, "adopt" some from flea markets or estate sales.*

Joseph. [Heb.] He shall add.—Dim.
Joe.

and

Margaret. [Gr.] A pearl.—Dim.
Greta, Mag, Madge, Maggie, Mar-
gie, Marjory, Meg, Meta, Peg.

ARTIST: *Linda O'Brien*

mailable photo note cards *These*

note cards are the perfect combination of card and gift. They are not only mailable, but also magnetic: you can make a card and send it through the mail to your aunt or your sister-in-law, and she can remove the magnet and put it on her refrigerator to hold artwork or recipes. Perfect!

1 Stamp images on glossy paper with permanent black ink.

2 Trim the paper, and then laminate the fronts and apply magnetic sheeting to the back. (This is easiest to do with a Zyron machine, but you can do it all by hand.)

3 Use the tin snips to cut a rectangle from the roofing tin, just a little larger all around than the laminated images. File the edges to smooth them.

4 Drill a hole in each corner of the roofing tin.

5 Lay the tin over the note card, and use the pencil to mark the holes. Punch holes in the note card.

6 Attach the tin to the note card with the eyelets, one in each hole. Set with the setting tool.

7 Place the magnet on the tin.

8 Embellish the card as desired.

MATERIALS

- galvanized roofing tin
- blank note cards
- four 1/8" (3 mm) short eyelets
- eyelet setter
- glossy paper
- photo rubber stamps
- permanent ink
- drill with 1/8" (3 mm) bit
- pencil
- awl or 1/8"(3 mm) paper punch
- hammer
- metal file
- laminating sheets
- magnetic sheets

TIP

- *Add captions to your cards with words and phrases that you have cut from old, discarded books—textbooks are especially fun for this—or simply stamp captions below the photos.*

hand-carved stamp

This hand-carved stamp was made from a drawing the artist made of her beloved dog, Dottie. It's the perfect way to create a personal stamp that can be used in various projects. To make a stamp of a relative of either the two-legged or four-legged variety, make a simple sketch, and then photocopy it.

MATERIALS

- carving block
- toner photocopy of drawing
- sanding block and extra-fine sand paper
- carving tool
- fingernail polish remover containing acetone (or plain acetone)
- stamping inks
- scrap paper
- good quality printmaking paper
- cutting mat

1   Transfer the image to the block (see page 14).

2   Use the carving tool to carve away the nonprinting parts of the carving block. The lines will remain, and they will form the image when you print on paper.

3   Make test stampings on scrap paper as you go along, checking to see how much more of the block needs to be removed.

4   When the image prints the way you want it to, clean it and ink it carefully. If the image is large, you may want to use a brayer to get even ink coverage.

5   Stamp the image on good-quality printmaking paper. If the block is large and you've inked it with a brayer, lay it faceup on your work surface, and lay the paper over it. Rub the back of the paper with a baren (used to press paper) or a spoon, being careful not to shift the paper.

6   Separate the print block and paper, and allow the image to dry.

TIPS

- *Stendahl uses a linoleum cutter with replaceable blades. Some carvers find the pull-type Linozip blades easier to use, and others prefer using a craft knife. You can also use a Dremel tool, using the fine bits and the flex-shaft attachment for precision cutting. Experiment with tools until you find the ones that work best for you.*

- *You can carve actual erasers; many artists have created tiny alphabets on the erasers of standard #2 pencils.*

TiPS

- *The artist sewed the page signatures into the purple book using a simple running stitch, which couldn't be easier. The red book was sewn using "tire-tracks," which is a zigzag stitch explained in* Keith Smith's One-, Two-, and Three-Section Sewings: Non-Adhesive Bindings Volume II.

- *Stendahl lined the purple book with Fabriano Tiziano and the red book with Canson Mi-Tientes. She recommends creating the signatures out of good-quality paper that's suitable for the purpose of your book: watercolor paper for an art journal, good-quality writing paper for a written journal, or acid-free paper for a photograph album.*

- *To create the charms shown on the spines, see page 124.*

ARTIST: *Roslyn M. Stendahl*

beaded spine book with carved stamped inset

This beaded spine book incorporates the stamping created in the previous project—making a perfect family album, a book containing the biography of a family member, or a blank journal. The instructions provided by the artist are for creating the cover of the book; the signatures may be added by any method you want to use for bookbinding.

1   Decide the size and location of the window for the stamped image. Use the ruler or straight edge and craft knife to cut out this window in the matte board.

2   Lay the book cloth facedown on your work surface. Apply glue to the front of the matte board, and place it facedown on the back of the book cloth, on the left-hand side. Use a book press or put weights on the board, and let it dry.

3   With the book cloth still face down, carefully cut the cloth in the window by making four cuts—one from each corner of the window—toward the center. You will then have four triangular flaps. Pull up the flaps and glue them to the back of the mat board, pulling and smoothing each flap so that the edges of the window are clean and tight. Weight the board and allow to dry.

4   Position the stamping in the window and glue the edges in place. Weight this, and let it dry.

5   Apply glue to one side of the thin binder's board, and press it firmly to the back (not the book cloth side) of the mat board, matching up the edges. Quickly turn it over and carefully press the stamped image so that it adheres to the binder's board. Weight and dry.

6   Attach the spine board and thick binder's board to the book cloth. Allow two board thicknesses of space from each cover board to your spine edge. This is your hinge, and it allows the book to open and close easily. Turn and trim the edges of the book cloth and glue in place. Weight this, and allow to dry.

7   Prepare an end sheet of heavyweight paper that is 1/2" (1.2 cm) less wide and 1/2" (1.2 cm) less tall than the entire cover (the spine and both boards). Apply glue to the back of this sheet, and place it on the inside of the cover boards. Smooth out any creases and ease the paper into the hinge with the bone folder. Weight this, and allow to dry.

8   Sew in the signatures using whatever method you prefer.

MATERIALS

- thick and thin binder's board
- matte board
- spine board (same thickness as the thick binder's board)
- book cloth
- PVA glue
- bristle brush or foam roller
- ruler
- craft knife
- weights or book press
- paper for book pages
- needle and thread (for sewing pages into book)

Note: The thick binder's board is for the back cover and spine, and the thin binder's board and matte board will make up the front cover. The latter two should, when placed together, equal the thickness of the thick binder's board. The book cloth will cover both the front and back of the book and so should be double the width of the boards, plus enough to allow for the spine and to wrap around all edges of the cover.

shrink plastic beads

After sewing in the signatures in the book on pages 122 and 123, you'll have some sort of stitching exposed on the spine. Those stitches are the perfect anchor for beading—from peyote stitch to fringe beading, whatever kind you like to do. To complement that beading, you can create your own beads out of shrink plastic. How else would you get these paw-print beads in exactly the right colors?

MATERIALS

- transparent shrink plastic
- fine-grit sandpaper
- stamping inks
- stamps
- 1/8" (3 mm) hole punch
- oven, toaster oven, or heat tool
- sealer (optional)
- thread
- needle

1 Sand the shrink plastic, both horizontally and vertically, to roughen the surface so that it will hold the ink.

2 Smear three colors of permanent dye ink on the surface. Use those same three colors to stamp a random background pattern on the plastic.

3 Use an alphabet stamp to stamp the title or label in black. You'll have to test a few of the letters to see how much they shrink and if they'll still be legible after shrinking. Stamp any other images that you want to shrink, using the black ink.

4 Punch a hole in each piece.

5 Shrink the plastic, following the manufacturer's instructions.

6 For the embossed charms, press your rubber stamp into the plastic after the piece is shrunken, but while the plastic is still soft. If your plastic has cooled, simply reheat it. (*Note:* To make it easier to release the stamp from the cooling plastic, you can first stamp into an embossing ink pad and then onto the soft plastic.)

7 If your project will get a lot of use, spray the cooled charms with sealer.

TIPS

- Rub permanent ink on embossed charms to make the image show up better.
- Punch holes at each end of the charm before shrinking so that once they're sewn on you can attach a smaller charm or bead to the bottom.

"a sailor's wedding" shrine

With a stamp made from a special family photo and a collection of memorabilia, you can construct a shrine that's not only a work of art but also a treasured keepsake that can be passed down to future generations. This wedding shrine commemorates a happy occasion and is the perfect prompt for family stories.

MATERIALS

- vintage wooden box (cigar boxes are great for this)
- old building blocks
- wooden game pieces
- glossy paper
- screws
- wire
- paint: assorted colors (we used Lumiere)
- brush
- drill with small bit
- photo stamp (see Resources, pages 138 and 139)
- document ink
- encaustic wax: assorted colors
- wood-burning tool, or soldering iron with metal brush tip for applying wax
- number stamps
- crafter's ink
- dress-pattern tissue
- decoupage glue
- mulberry paper
- embellishments: family keepsakes, coins, jewelry, keys, old newspaper clippings

1 Construct the shrine using an old box and various children's building blocks. Attach these as needed with screws and wire, rather than glue. You can use decorative brass nails and screws in places where they will show.

2 Paint the shrine with several colors, and allow it to dry.

3 Enhance the surface with several colors of encaustic wax, applying it with the wood-burning tool or soldering iron with metal brush tip.

4 While the paint is drying, stamp the photo stamp on heavy, glossy paper with permanent ink. Allow it to dry.

5 Attach the stamped paper to a wooden block; a Zyron laminating machine is great for this, but you can use an adhesive, eyelets, or other creative attachment.

6 Stamp the numbers onto dress-pattern paper. Cut them out and adhere them to mulberry paper and then onto wooden game tiles. Attach these with wood glue or creative attachments.

7 Next is the fun part: finding creative ways to attach all the bits and pieces of memorabilia to your shrine. Metal pieces, like the 1944 quarter shown on the left, can be drilled and attached to wooden blocks with decorative brass screws. Other pieces can be wired or attached with eyelets and an eyelet setter.

TIPS

- *If you don't have a photo stamp, you can use a generic stamped image to represent family members or you could use a color copy or an actual photograph.*

- *Use a tiny alphabet to stamp the story of the photograph in the shrine. You could also stamp a poem, wedding vows, or the wording on an invitation.*

- *Wedding shrines are terrific anniversary gifts, and you can make them for newlyweds, too: incorporate the invitation and age all the pieces to make them look old.*

photo transfer shrine pin

Shrines are a wonderful way to honor someone close to you, and making a wearable shrine allows you to share your tribute whenever you wear it. Scan your stamped image into your computer to change the size, print it on transfer paper, and make the shrine whatever size you'd like—from small, pin-sized shrines to larger ornament shrines to even larger pillow-sized shrines. The doors are optional, and embellishments can take any form that appeals to you.

MATERIALS

- tea-dyed muslin
  (see pages 17 and 18)
- photo transfers
  (see pages 19 and 20)
- shrine stamp
- low-loft quilt batting
- matte board
- Ultrasuede
- seed beads
- gold beads
- fabric paint
- paintbrush
- needle
- thread
- pin back
- glue

1   Make photo transfers of both a family photo and the shrine stamp, adjusting the sizes so that the two work together. The shrine shown is approximately 2³/₄" × 3" (7 cm × 7.5 cm).

2   Cut the doors from the inside of the photo transfer of the shrine, and then cut them apart so that there are three shrine transfers: the body of the shrine and two separate doors. Iron each of these onto its own piece of tea-dyed muslin, leaving a large margin all around. Cut out, leaving the margin, and set the doors aside.

3   Replace the paper backing of the shrine to serve as a mask. Place the family photo transfer inside the opening and iron. Set aside.

4   To make the doors sturdy, place each one facedown on another piece of muslin, and sew around the edges, leaving most of one side open for turning. Trim the corners, turn right side out, and stitch closed. Press the edges flat, but don't iron over the transfer itself.

5   Trim the matte board to just slightly larger than the shrine. Lightly glue batting to the front, trimming the edges. Place the muslin with the transferred shrine over the batting, centering the transfer. Fold all edges to the back, overlapping and gluing in place. Allow to dry.

6   Cut Ultrasuede slightly smaller than the back of the shine. Sew on the pin back, and then glue the Ultrasuede in place. Allow to dry.

7   Use gold paint to highlight details on the front of the shrine. Sew on the beads and fringe. Attach doors with small stitches as "hinges."

TIPS

- *Sew tiny bells onto the bottom, instead of fringe.*

- *Use colored pencils or fabric markers to tint parts of the shrine.*

- *Use beads for door handles or buy tiny hardware from the dollhouse section of craft supply stores.*

TIPS

- *You can use an actual photograph rather than a stamped image, or a good-quality color copy.*
- *Drill holes along the bottom edge of the frame to attach beads after etching. You can attach charms or other keepsakes, as well.*

"meditate-communicate-advocate-love" pendant

To make this etched metal pendant, the artists used a photo stamp of Linda's Aunt Fran—a woman who, at 90, is still a mentor and advocate for her niece. The pendant incorporates her image with stamped words that evoke her inspirational attitude. See the Resources section on pages 138 and 139 for information about where to have stamps made from your family photos.

1 Cut two pieces of the copper. One will be the frame, and you can shape it however you wish. The other piece will be the back; make it slightly smaller.

2 To cut the window, drill a hole into the middle of the frame and insert the blade of the jeweler's saw. Cut the window. File all rough edges with the metal file, and then sand the surfaces in a circular motion, using the sandpaper.

3 Using the 1/8" (3 mm) drill bit, drill two holes in the upper corners of the frame to attach the jump rings for the chain or cord. Using the 1/16" (2 mm) drill bit, drill four holes in the frame and four corresponding holes in the back piece. You'll attach these two pieces after etching.

4 Tape the backs of both pieces with the masking tape, covering the entire surface and pressing the tape firmly in place.

5 Ink the stamps with Memories black ink and stamp the metal. Allow the ink to dry completely.

6 Wearing rubber gloves, pour etching solution in a container large enough to allow the metal pieces to lie flat, without overlapping, and to be covered with the solution (see page 21). Use the tongs to place the metal in the solution. Cover and check after two hours. The pendant shown here took six hours to etch. When the metal has etched as much as you want it to, put on the rubber gloves, and use the tongs to remove the metal from the solution. Rinse it thoroughly under running water.

7 Remove the tape from the backs, and clean them with alcohol.

8 Stamp the photo stamp on glossy paper and laminate it.

9 Sandwich the stamped image between the two pieces of metal, and secure them with the four 1/16" (2 mm) eyelets. Set with the eyelet setter. Insert the 1/8" (3 mm) short eyelets in the top two holes in the frame. Set with the eyelet setter, and attach the jump rings and ball chain or cord.

MATERIALS

- 18-gauge copper
- masking tape
- jump rings
- eyelets: two 1/8" (3 mm); four 1/16" (2 mm)
- ball chain or silk cord
- drill with 1/8" (3 mm); four 1/16" (2 mm) drill bit
- metal shears for cutting
- mallet or hammer with rubber head
- eyelet setter
- metal file
- sandpaper
- alcohol
- PCB Etchant Solution (available from Radio Shack)
- art stamps
- photo stamp
- glossy paper
- Memories Ink: black (other inks won't work)
- plastic or glass container with a cover
- disposable rubber gloves
- tweezers or tongs
- needle-nosed pliers
- matte sealer
- access to a laminating machine

"my people" photograph album

Rather than displaying old family photographs in a plain purchased album, you can create your own. This simple portfolio is quick and easy to make, so you can create individual albums for each set of photographs. Use good-quality color copies or original photographs; if you use photos, invest in acid-free papers and adhesives. Whatever you choose, you'll have a way to display and share photographs of the people you hold in your heart.

MATERIALS

- family photographs or good-quality color copies (optional)
- color transparency of photographs
- card stock
- regular weight paper
- shipping tag
- ribbon
- button
- vintage book
- gold-leafing pen
- hole punch
- dye-based ink
- art stamps
- adhesive

1　Fold the card stock in half and trim to desired size.

2　For the outside cover, stamp the shipping tag, and color the edges with the gold-leafing pen. Attach the button to the tag.

3　Trim the transparency, and attach it to the shipping tag.

4　Layer several pieces of card stock, and attach with adhesive.

5　For the inside, fold and score a slightly smaller piece of the same card stock. Center it and attach with adhesive.

6　Stamp mattes for the photographs, and layer them on pieces of card stock.

7　For one photograph, create a tag of the black card stock. Punch a hole and attach the ribbon, and then layer this tag with stamped paper and the photograph.

8　Cut a poem from the book or make a photocopy. Age it by tea-dying or sponging with sepia ink. Cut the words apart, and glue them to the card stock separately.

The night is beautiful
So the faces
of my people

The stars are beautiful
So the eyes
of my people

Beautiful also is the sun.
Beautiful also are the souls
of my people

LANGSTON HUGHES

TIPS

- *You can create multiple pages by sewing in more sheets of card stock, or you can attach smaller booklets inside this portfolio. Be creative in adding layers and pages.*

- *Embellish the outside with bits of trim or fabric, beads or more buttons.*

- *Create labels for the photographs on the computer. Print these out onto sepia paper (or age your own paper).*

- *Make a title for your album, or add a poem like the one here by Langston Hughes.*

PATTERNS AND ILLUSTRATIONS

Iris Tattoo Journal Skirt, pages 42 and 43

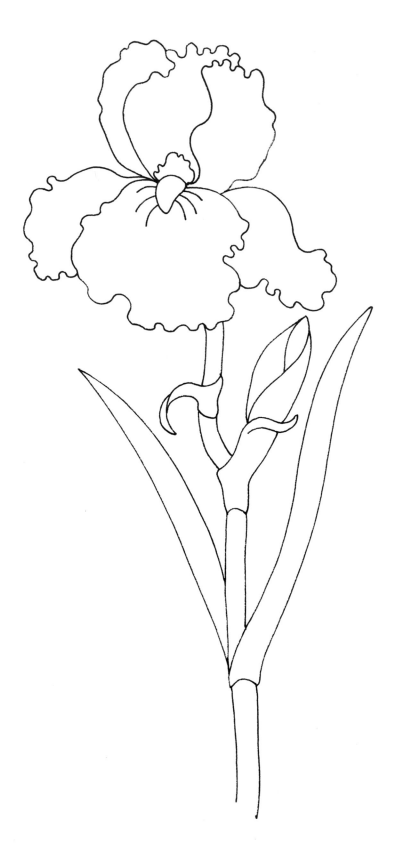

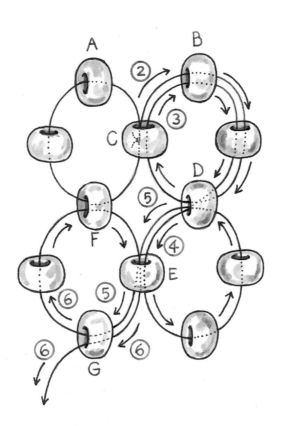

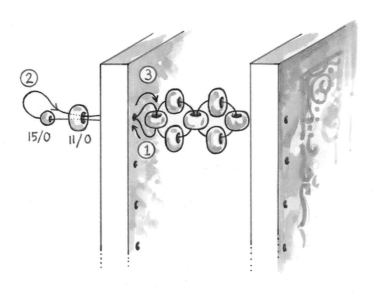

DIRECTORY OF ARTISTS

NANETTE ALEXANDER
pp. 114, 132
Chicago, IL

Nanette Alexander is an artist and actor who has studied classical theater in London and New York. A frequent contributor to *Rubberstampmadness,* her artwork was featured on the cover of their 2002 photos issue. Her work has also appeared in *The Rubber Stamper* and *Somerset Studio Gallery.*

BABETTE K. COX
pp. 62, 70, 92, 98
Dallas, TX
www.createdbybabette.com
babette1@earhtlink.net

As an artist, Babette K. Cox has been working with crafts for more than 25 years. She exhibits locally and teaches nationally as a certified professional demonstrator (CPD) and teacher (CPT), and her artwork has appeared in books and many crafting magazines. As the owner of Digit Designs, she is a professional digitizer and converts graphic designs to embroidery for wearable goods in the corporate sportswear industry.

TERRY GARRETT
pp. 96, 102
Bemidji, MN
Phone: (218) 759-6991
www.gallery.passion4art.com/
    members/creekside/index.html
tgarrett@paulbunyan.net

Terry Garrett is a collage artist, photographer, and bookmaker living in northern Minnesota. His work has been published in several magazines and has been featured in exhibitions around the country. His use of his own photographic imagery in his collages makes his work unique.

DONNA GOSS
pp. 64, 100, 108
Rowlett, TX

Donna Goss enjoys sharing her artistic skills through the development of advanced stamp art classes and continues to search out and master all kinds of mixed media. Her art has been published in the *Stampers Sampler, Somerset Studio Gallery* and various scrapbooking magazines.

COREY HEIMKE
p. 86
Redmond, WA
appendageassemblage@hotmail.com

Corey Heimke is an artist who works primarily with collage. She loves the harmony that is created when bits and pieces of unrelated "stuff" come together into a perfect blend of composition, color, and meaning. She comes from a background in art therapy, so she believes that art is as much about the instinctual process as the beautiful end result.

SUSAN LENART KAZMER
p. 74
Vermilion, OH
Phone: (440) 967.9654
www.susanlenartkazmer.net
slnartkazmer@aldelphia.net

Susan Lenart Kazmer is an artist and award-winning jewelry designer. She also teaches nationally. Her recent work, in metals and found objects, has been involved in a number of museum exhibits.

PEGGY M. KOOP
pp. 32, 36, 90
Minneapolis, MN
Phone: (952) 474-4257
www.artclayworld.com/
    instructors.html

A certified senior instructor in Art Clay Silver, Peggy M. Koop is a mixed-media artist who teaches workshops in a variety of mediums. She finds the versatility of fine silver and gold clay enrapturing and surprising in its enrich-ments of pieces involving bookmaking, rubber stamping, sculpting, twining, braiding, wire coiling, beading, warm glass fusing, lampworking, silver-smithing, polymer clay molding, and crocheting. She holds a BA degree from the University of Minnesota, with a major in English creative writing and minor in fine arts.

LINDA O'BRIEN
pp. 28, 34, 68, 118, 126, 130
N. Perry Village, OH
www.burntofferings.com

Linda O'Brien is a mixed-media artist, writer, and jewelry and stamp designer whose work has appeared in several publications, gallery shows, and museum exhibits. She teaches workshops nationwide using organic, recycled, and found materials and is the co-owner of Burnt Offerings.

OPIE O'BRIEN
pp. 58, 68, 126, 130
N. Perry Village, OH
www.burntofferings.com

Opie O'Brien is a mixed-media artist, musician, and jewelry and stamp designer whose work has been shown in galleries, solo shows, museum exhibits, and several publications. He teaches workshops nationwide using organic, recycled, and found materials and is the co-owner of Burnt Offerings.

LYNNE PERRELLA
p. 80
Ancram, NY
www.lkperrella.com

Lynne Perrella is an illustrator, mixed-media artist, writer, and teacher. She is the owner of Acey Deucy Rubber Stamps and makes regular contributions to various paper arts publications and books. Her main interest, art-wise, is in forms of layering, including collage and assemblage, one-of-a-kind books, and journals.

LISA RENNER
pp. 26, 44
McKinney, TX
lisarenner@attbi.com

Lisa Renner is a mixed-media paper artist whose range of interests includes textural collage, jewelry, polymer clay, bookbinding, and Cigar Box Purses (which she sells in boutiques). Her work has been published in magazines, including *Stamper's Sampler, Somerset Studio Gallery, Belle Armoire,* and in the following books: *Stamp Art* by Sharilyn Miller, *The Art of Paper Collage* by Susan Pickering Rothamel, and *True Colors,* published by Stampington and Co. She teaches classes at rubber-stamp stores and conventions, incorporating rubber stamps as vital tools in mixed media art.

JUDI RIESCH
p. 116
Philadelphia, PA
itsmysite.com/judiriesch
JJRiesch@aol.com

Judi Riesch is a mixed-media artist working primarily in collage and assemblage. Her boxes, books, and collage work feature fragments from the past and, often, her own Polaroid image transfers. They have been seen in galleries, paper arts publications, and art books.

ANNE SAGOR
pp. 46, 50, 60, 72, 82, 88, 106
Garland, TX
sooie@juno.com

From childhood on, Anne Sagor has been involved with arts and crafts. Her current artistic passions center around rubber stamping and paper arts. She creates samples for several major rubber stamp companies and teaches at Stamp Asylum in Plano, Texas.

ALLENE SHACKELFORD
p. 52
Healdsburg, CA
Phone: (707) 431-1400
www.toyboxart.com

Allene Shackelford is the owner/artist of Toybox Rubber Stamps. Her techniques and unique artwork have been featured in many publications, books, and videos. Allene's background also includes teaching, quilting, stamping, and jewelry making. She is currently working on her second book for Toybox.

ROSLYN M. STENDAHL
pp. 84, 120, 122, 124
Minneapolis, MN
www.rozworks.com
roz@rozworks.com

Roslyn M. Stendahl is a graphic designer, illustrator, and writer. She has been keeping visual and written journals since childhood. She teaches book arts, journaling, and art classes.

DOROTHEA TORTILLA
pp. 78, 104
Bandon, OR
Phone: (800) 366-7416
dorotheatortilla@msn.com

Dorothea Tortilla has worked with leather and beads for over 25 years. She owns her own business: Poor Taste, a source for campy, offbeat creations and fine leatherwork.

MICHELLE WARD
p. 24
Piscataway, NJ
www.greenpepperpress.com
grnpep@ontoline.net

Michelle Ward is an artist of mixed media, primarily paper arts. She designs rubber stamps for her own company, Green Pepper Press, and for Stampington & Company. Michelle teaches workshops from her studio in New Jersey.

LINDA WOODS
pp. 30, 48
Valencia, CA
www.colormetrue.com
www.sistersonsojourn.com

Linda Woods is a mixed media artist whose works have appeared in numerous publications. Her stamp art, collages, and assemblages are in collections all over the world. Linda's love of art and travel inspired the works featured on her Web sites.

RESOURCES

NORTH AMERICA

ABOVE THE MARK
P.O. Box 8307
Woodland, CA 95776
Phone: (530) 666-6648
www.abovethemark.com

ACEY DEUCY
P.O. Box 194
Ancram, NY 12502
Phone: (518) 398-5108
Fax: (518) 398-6364

ALL NIGHT MEDIA
www.allnightmedia.com

ANN-TICIPATIONS
6507 Pacific Avenue
Stockton, CA 95207
Phone: (209) 952-5538
Fax: (209) 952-4579

BIZARRO
P.O. Box 292
Greenville, RI 02828
Phone: (401) 231-8777
Fax: (401) 231-4770
www.bizarro.com

BURNT OFFERINGS
Opie and Linda O'Brien
2170 Evergreen Road
N. Perry Village, OH 44081-7603
Phone/fax: (440) 259-2271
www.burntofferings.com

CHARACTER CONSTRUCTIONS
224 Melrah Hill
Peachtree City, GA 30269
Phone: (770) 632-9570
Fax: (770) 632-0416
www.ItsMySite.com/CatherineMoore

CIRCUSTAMPS
Jim Marcus
P.O Box 250
Bolinas, CA 94924
Phone: (415) 868-1470
Fax: (415) 868-1939
jimmarcus@circustamps.com

CREATIVE BLOCK
STAMPERS ANONYMOUS
2567 Detroit Road
Weslake, OH 44145
Phone/Fax: (440) 25-9112
www.stampersanonymous.com

DENAMI DESIGN
RUBBER STAMPS
Phone: (253) 437-1626
Fax: (253) 437-1627
www.denamidesign.com

ECLECTIC OMNIBUS
P.O. Box 6768
Glendale, AZ 85312
Phone: (602) 524-7951
Fax: (602) 564-0135
www.ajsstampworld.com

FRED B. MULLETT
RUBBER STAMPS
P.O. Box 94502
Seattle, WA 98124
Phone: (206) 624-5723
Fax: (206) 903-8202
www.fredbmullett.com

FRUIT BASKET UPSET
1248 9th Avenue
San Francisco, CA 94122
Phone: (415) 566-1018
Fax: (415) 566-6696
www.stampfrancisco.com

GOOD STAMPS STAMP GOODS
30901 Timberline Road
Willits, CA 95490
Phone: (800) 637-6401
Fax: (707) 459-5021
www.rubberstampgoods.com

GREEN PEPPER PRESS
P.O. Box 73
Piscataway, NJ 08855-0073
www.greenpepperpress.com

GUMBO GRAPHICS
1320 N.W. Northrup Street
Portland, OR 97209
Phone: (503) 223-2824

HERO ARTS
1343 Powell Street
Emeryville, CA 94608
Phone: (800) 822-4376
Fax: (800) 441-3632
www.heroarts.com

HOMEWARD COLLECTION
see Green Pepper Press

INKADINKADO
60 Cummings Park
Woburn, MA 01801
Phone: (781) 938-6100
Fax: (781) 938-5585
www.inkadinkado.com

IVORY COAST TRADING POSTE
1248 9th Avenue
San Francisco, CA 94122
Phone: (415) 566-1018
Fax: (415) 566-6696
www.stampfrancisco.com

JUDIKINS
17832 South Harvard Boulevard
Gardena, CA 90248
Phone: (310) 515-1115
Fax: (310) 323-6619
www.judikins.com

JUNQUE
P.O. Box 2378
Providence, RI 02906
www.junque.net

JUST FOR FUN RUBBER STAMPS
301 E. Lemon Street, Suite A-B
Tarpon Spring, FL 34689
Phone: (727) 938-9898
Fax: (727) 938-7600
www.jffstamps.com

LEAVENWORTH JACKSON
P.O. Box 9988
Berkeley, CA 94709
www.ljackson.com

LIMITED EDITION
1011 Bransten Road, Suite C
San Carlos, CA 94070
Toll-Free: (877) 9-STAMPS
Fax: (650) 632-2711
Wholesale only: (888) STAMP-98
www.limitededitionrs.com

A LOST ART
P.O. Box 1338
Baldwin Park, CA 91706
Phone: (818) 790-2125
Fax: (909) 592-3067

MA VINCI'S RELIQUARY
P.O. Box 472702
Aurora, CO 80047-2702
MVReliquary@juno.com
www.crafts.dm.net/mall/reliquary/

MAGENTA STYLE
2275 Bombardier
Sainte-Julie QC J3E 2J9 Canada
Phone: (450) 922-5253
Fax: (450) 922-0053
www.magentastyle.com

MARKS OF DISTINCTION
10 West North Avenue
Chicago, IL 60622-2553
Phone: (312) 335-9266
www.marksofdistinction.com

MODERN ILLUMINATOR
P.O. Box 8555
Berkeley, CA 94707
www.modernilluminator.com

MOON ROSE
P.O. Box 833
Yaphank, NY 11980
Phone: (516) 549-0199
Fax: (516) 924-7292

NON SEQUITUR
2602 Florence Avenue
Pasadena, TX 77502-3245
Fax: (713) 475-9506
www.nonsequiturstamps.com

OM STUDIO
P.O. Box 448
Seaside, OR 97138
Phone: (800) 738-6955

100 PROOF PRESS
P.O. Box 299
Athens, OH 45701
Phone: 740) 594-2315
Fax: (800) 511-210
www.100proofpress.com

ORNAMENTUM
20611 E Bothell Everett Highway
Bothell, WA 98012
Phone: (425) 481-6509

OUR LADY OF RUBBER
P.O. Box 1892
Bisbee, AZ 85603

PAULA BEST
507 Trail Drive
Moss Landing, CA 95039
www.paulabest.com
paulabest@earthlink.net

PERSONAL STAMP EXCHANGE
360 Sutton Place
Santa Rosa, CA 95407
Phone: (707) 588-8058
Wholesale only
Fax: (707) 588-7476
www.psxdesign.com

PLAID (SIMPLY STAMPS)
3225 Westech Drive
Norcross, GA 30092-350
Phone: (800) 842-4197
www.plaidonline.com

POSH IMPRESSIONS
22600 Lambert Street, Suite 706
Lake Forest, CA 92630
Phone: (800) 421-POSH (7674)
Fax: (800) 422-POSH (7674)
www.poshimpressions.com

POSTMODERN DESIGN
P.O. Box 720416
Norman, OK 73070
Phone: (405) 321-3176

RED PEARL
P.O. Box 94502
Seattle, WA 98124
Phone: (206) 624-5723
Fax: (206) 903-8202

RENAISSANCE ART STAMPS
P.O. Box 1218
Burlington, CT 06013
Phone/Fax: (860) 485-7761

RIVER CITY RUBBER WORKS
5555 South Meridian
Wichita, KS 67217
Phone: (316) 529-8656
Fax: (316) 529-8940
www.rivercityrubberworks.com

RUBBER POET
1213 Glenmore Avenue
Baton Rouge, LA 70806-7029
Phone/Fax: (800) 906-POET
www.rubberpoet.com

RUBBER STAMPEDE
P.O. Box 246
Berkeley, CA 94701
Phone: (510) 420-6831
www.deltacrafts.com

RUBBER STAMPS OF AMERICA
160 Emerald Street
Keene, NH 03431
Phone: (800) 553-5031
Fax: (603) 352-0265
www.stampusa.com

RUBBERMOON
P.O. Box 3258
Hayden Lake, ID 83835
Phone: (208) 772-9772
Fax: (208) 772-0701
www.rubbermoon.com

RUBBERNECKER
932 Laroda Court
Ontario, CA 91762
Phone: (909) 673-0747

SISTERS ON SOJOURN
www.sistersonsojourn.com

STAMP FRANCISCO
308 SE 271st Court
Camas, WA 98607
Phone: (360) 210-4031
Toll-Free Fax Order: (877) 268-4869
Other Fax: (360) 210-4037
www.stampfrancisco.com

A STAMP IN THE HAND
20630 S. Leapwood Avenue, Suite B
Carson, CA 90746
Phone: (310) 329-8555
www.astampinthehand.com

STAMP OASIS
4750 West Sahara Avenue, Suite 17
Las Vegas, NV 89102
Phone: (702) 878-6474
Fax: (702) 878-7824
www.stampoasis.com

STAMP OUT CUTE
7084 North Cedar #137
Fresno, CA 93720
Phone/Fax: (559) 323-7174
www.stampoutcute.com

STAMPERS ANONYMOUS
20613 Center Ridge Road
Rocky River, OH 44116
Phone: (440) 333-7941
Fax: (440) 333-7992
www.stampersanonymous.com

THE STAMPING GROUND
15B Otis Street
W. Babylon, NY 11704
Phone: (631) 643-3100
Fax: (631) 643-6812
info@stampingground.com
Stamps made from photographs

STAMPINGTON & COMPANY
22992 Mill Creek, Suite B
Laguna Hills, CA 92653
Phone: (949) 380-7318
Fax: (949) 380-9355
www.stampington.com

STAMPLAND
5033 No. Mozart Street
Chicago, IL 60625
Phone/Fax: (773) 293-0404
www.Stamplandchicago.com

STAMPSCAPES
10820 Beverly Boulevard
A5 PMB 342
Whittier, CA 90601
Fax: (562) 695-5905
www.stampscapes.com

TOO MUCH FUN RUBBER STAMPS
P.O. Box 4306
Hampton, VA 23664
Phone: (757) 851-0715
Fax: (757) 851-0716
www.toomuchfunrubberstamps.com

TOYBOX RUBBER STAMPS
P.O. Box 1487
Healdsburg, CA 95448
Phone: (707) 431-1400
Fax: (707) 431-2408
www.toyboxart.com

THE TURTLE PRESS STUDIO
AND STORE
2215 NW Market Street
Seattle, WA 98107
www.turtlearts.com

UPTOWN RUBBER STAMPS
315 West Hickory Street
Fort Collins, CO 80524-1100
Phone: (800) 888-3212
Fax: (800) 466-9515
www.uptownrubberstamps.com

VIVA LAS VEGASTAMPS!
1008 East Sahara Avenue
Las Vegas, NV 89104
www.stampo.com

ZETTIOLOGY ALTERNATIVE ARTS
P.O. Box 3329
Renton, WA 98056
Fax: (425) 271-5506
www.zettiology.com

ZIMPRINTS
7121 Merrick Drive SW
Knoxville, TN 37919-8119
Phone/Fax: (865) 584-9430
www.zimprints.com

INK COMPANIES

CLEARSNAP
Phone: (800) 448-4862
www.clearsnap.com

DR. PH. MARTIN'S
(Salis International)
(800) 843-8293
www.docmartins.com
docmartins@docmartins.com

MARVY UCHIDA
Phone: (800) 541-5877
www.uchida.com

RANGER INDUSTRIES, INC.
Phone: (800) 244-2211
Fax: (800) 266-1397
www.rangerink.com

STEWART SUPERIOR
www.stewartsuperior.com

TSUKINEKO
Phone: (800) 769-6633
www.tsukineko.com

OTHER SUPPLIES

ARNOLD GRUMMER
(800) 453-1485
www.arnoldgrummer.com
Papermaking supplies galore

BONNIE'S BEST
3314 Inman Drive NE
Atlanta, GA 30319-2428
Phone: (404) 869-0081
www.coilconnection.com
bonnie@coilconnection.com
Art supplies and goodies

BURNT OFFERINGS
2170 Evergreen Road
N. Perry Village, OH 44081
(440) 259-2271
www.burntofferings.com
gourdart@burntofferings.com
Unmounted rubber and artwork

COFFEE BREAK DESIGN
P.O. Box 34281
Indianapolis, IN 46234
Phone: (317) 290-1542
Fax: (317) 293-1824
Eyelets, fasteners, and creative
necessities

DHARMA TRADING COMPANY
Phone: (800) 542-5227
www.dharmatrading.com
Fabric art supplies, from paint to
dye to silk blanks

ELOXITE
P.O. Box 729
Wheatland, WY 82201
www.eloxite.net
Jewelry parts; bracelet blank

INKFLUENCE TATTOOS
Mike Tweed
www.313tattoo.com
Iris pattern, page 134

NASCO
Phone: (800) 558-9595
www.enasco.com
Carving blocks, art supplies

RIO GRANDE
Phone: (800) 545-6566
www.riogrande.com
Everything you need for making
jewelry

THAI SILKS!
252 State Street
Los Altos, CA 94022
www.thaisilks.com
Silk clothing blanks

UNCLE WALTER'S
CARVING BLOCK
P.O. Box 35
Amesbury, MA 01913
Phone (978) 388-2020

UK AND EUROPE

CHERRY PIE ART
Via Antica Romana
33A/4, 16166 Quinto al Mare
Genova Italy
www.cherrypie.theshoppe.com

CREATIVE CRAFTS
11 The Square Winchester,
Hampshire SO23 9ES
United Kingdom
Phone: 01962 856266
www.creativecrafts.co.uk

HEINDESIGN
Expressby Road 76
58091 Hagen Germany
Phone: (49) 0 23 32/7 22 11
Fax: (49) 0 23 31/7 22 92
www.heindesign.de

HOBBYCRAFT
Head Office
Bournemouth United Kingdom
Phone: 1202 596 100
Stores throughout the UK

JOHN LEWIS
Flagship Store
Oxford Street, London W1A 1EX
United Kindgom
Phone: 207 629 7711
www.johnlewis.co.uk
Stores throughout the UK

T N LAWRENCE & SON LTD.
208 Portland Road
Hove BN3 5QT United Kingdom
Phone: 0845 644 3232
www.lawerence.co.uk
artbox@lawrence.co.uk

Australia and New Zealand

ANNALEEY CRAFTS
P.O. Box 66
Yeelanna SA 5632
Phone: 08 8676 5026
Stamps@Annaleeycrafts.Com.Au

AUSSIE STAMPS & CRAFTS
4 Brougham Place
Golden Grove SA 5125
Phone: 08 82898871
Mwo@Iweb.Net.Au

BLACK CAT CREATIONS
P.O. Box 489
Everton Park QLD 4053
Phone: 07 3354 4411

BUMBLE BEE CRAFTS
7 Toolara Street
The Gap QLD 4061
Phone: 07 3511 0068
Buzz@Gil.Com.Au

CAMBRAE STAMPS
Shop 36, The Gateway Village
230 Cranbourne Road
Langwarrin VIC 3910
Phone: 03 8790 8217
Cambraestamps@Netstra.Com.Au

COLLECTIONS RUBBER STAMPS
6 Alisa Court
Alexander Heights WA 6064
Phone: 08 9247-3665

CREATIVE ART STAMPS
399 Honour Avenue
Graceville QLD 4075
Phone: 07 3278 2814

**THE CREATIVE STAMP
COLLECTION PTY LTD**
6-10 Kepple Street
Shepparton VIC 3630
Phone: 03 5831 3233

DEEP IMPRESSIONS
1/38 Nepean Avenue
Moorabbin VIC 3189
Phone: 03 9773 5889
Impressions@Hotvoice.Com

DREAM MODE
P.O. Box 338
Tailem Bend SA 5260
Phone: 08 85723553

**ECKERSLEY'S ARTS, CRAFTS,
AND IMAGINATION**
(store locations in New South
Wales, Queensland, South Australia,
and Victoria)
Phone for catalog: (300) 657-766
www.eckersleys.com.au

ELIZABETH LEE COUNTRY STAMPS
42 Phillipson Road
Charters Towers QLD 4820
Phone: 07 4787 3712

FANTASY CRAFT STAMPS
224 Brunker Road
Adamstown NSW 2289
Phone: 02 4957 2255

GAIL'S STAMPS & CRAFTS
22 Binney Street
Ravenswood TAS 7250
Phone: 03 6339 2002
Fsargent@Our.Net.Au

HANDSTAMPED ART
P.O. Box 439n
North Cairns QLD 4870
Phone: 07 4057 5812
Handstamped@iig.Com.Au

IMPRESSIVE STAMPS AUSTRALIA
13 Agnew Street
Norman Park QLD 4170
Phone: 07 3399 3737
Berni@Tpg.Com.Au

LITTLE BITS
389 Chandler Road
Keysborough VIC 3173
Phone: 03 9798 4122

**LITTLEJOHNS ART & GRAPHIC
SUPPLIES LTD**
170 Victoria Street
Wellington New Zealand
Phone: 04 385 2099
Fax: 04 385 2090

LUCY'S STAMPS
30 Macaranga Street
Marsden QLD 4132
Phone: 07 3805 1115

MY STAMPING GROUND
Top Of The Town
Shop 3/133 Princes Hwy
Ulladulla NSW 2539
Phone: 02 4454 3260

**PLATYPUS CREEK STAMPING
& CRAFT**
Shop 3 Stanto Place
(Cnr Stanton Rd & Captain Cook Hwy)
Smithfield QLD
Phone: 07 4038 1013
Platycreek@Bigpond.com

RIVENDELL COTTAGE
109 Ryrie Street
Geelong VIC 3220
Phone: 03 5224 1911

THE RUBBER STAMP COMPANY
Shop 4, 1919 Albany Highway
Maddington WA 6109
Phone: 08 9493 2730

THE RUBBER STAMP SHOP
37 Beach Street
Wollongong NSW 2500
Phone: 02 4229 6594
Imprint@Ho000ey.Net.Au

SOUTH WEST RUBBER STAMPS
Shop 9 Koombana Court
141 Victoria Street
Bunbury WA 6230
Phone: 08 9791 5050

STAMP IN STYLE
376 Forest Road
Bexley NSW 2207
Phone: 02 9597 2676
Stampinstyle@Optusnet.Com.Au

STAMPALOT
Cnr Main & Barkly Streets
Mornington VIC 3931
Phone: 03 5975 8550

STAMP-IT RUBBER STAMPS
276 Albany Highway
Victoria Park WA 6100
Phone: 08 9470 5422
Stamps@Stampit.Com.Au

A STAMPER'S FRIEND
16 Foothill Street
Elanora QLD 4221
Phone: 07 5534 6506
Sharmies@One.Net.Au

THE STAMPERS GARAGE
50 Anchorage Street
Erskine Park NSW 2759
Phone: 02 8803 0896
Thestampersgarage@Goconnect.Net

STAMPERS HEAVEN
Shop 5
257 Stafford Road
Stafford QLD 4053
Phone: 07 3857 7799

THE STAMPING BUG GIFT SHOP
Shop 8/39 Wragg Street
Somerset TAS 7322
Phone: 03 6435 0603
Stampingbug@Bigpond.Com.Au

STAMPMANIA
Shop 6 Alexandria Street
Berry NSW 2535
Phone: 02 4464 2677
Stampmania@Shoal.Net.Au

Magazines

ART DOLL QUARTERLY
22992 Mill Creek, Suite B
Laguna Hills, CA 92653
Phone: (949) 380-7318
Fax: (949) 380-9355
www.stampington.com

BELLE ARMOIRE
22992 Mill Creek, Suite B
Laguna Hills, CA 92653
Phone: (949) 380-7318
Fax: (949) 380-9355
www.stampington.com

CANADIAN STAMPER
922 Alder Avenue
Sherwood Park, AB T8A 1V6 Canada
Phone: (780) 467-4443
info@canadianstamper.ca
www.canadianstamper.ca

CRAFT STAMPER MAGAZINE
www.traplet.com/stamp
general@traplet.com

INSPIRATIONS
22992 Mill Creek, Suite B
Laguna Hills, CA 92653
Phone: (949) 380-7318
Fax: (949) 380-9355
www.stampington.com

THE RUBBER GAZETTE
6 Ailsa Court
Alexander Heights
Western Australia 6064
lea@bigpond.net.au

RUBBERSTAMPMADNESS
P.O. Box 610
Corvallis, OR 97339-0610
Phone: (877) STAMPMA (782-6762)
Fax: (541) 752-5475
www.rsmadness.com
rsm@rsmadness.com

SOMERSET STUDIO
22992 Mill Creek, Suite B
Laguna Hills, CA 92653
Phone: (949) 380-7318
Fax: (949) 380-9355
www.stampington.com

STAMPERS' SAMPLER
22992 Mill Creek, Suite B
Laguna Hills, CA 92653
Phone: (949) 380-7318
Fax: (949) 380-9355
www.stampington.com

STAMPING & PAPERCRAFTS
Express Publications Pty, Ltd.
Reply Paid 60476
Silverwater, NSW 2128, Australia
www.isubscribe.com.au/title_info.
    cfm?prodID=161
subs@expresspublications.com.au

STAMP CREDITS

FOR THE HOME

"A CLOWN'S KISS," p. 24
  Stampers Anonymous

"BLOCKHEAD" PENHOLDER & PEN, p. 26
  Acey Deucy
  Rubber Gems
  A Stamp in the Hand
  Stampers Anonymous
  Zettiology

RUBBER-STAMPED GOURD VESSELS, p. 28
  Acey Deucy
  Burnt Offerings
  Non Sequitur
  A Stamp in the Hand
  Stampers Anonymous
  Stampington and Co.

FUNKY LAZY SUSAN, p. 30
  stamps cut from Fun Foam

SILVER PINCUSHION, p. 32
  JudiKins

"EXPECTING A MIRACLE" PICTURE FRAME, p. 34
  Burnt Offerings

STAMPED SILVER ORNAMENT, p. 36
  Rubber Stampede

COVERED CLOTHES
  HANGERS, p. 38
  Simply Stamps (Plaid)
  Sisters on Sojourn

FOR THE BODY

IRIS-TATTOO JOURNAL SKIRT, p. 42
  hand-carved iris
  Stamp Out Cute alphabet

COLLAGED AND STAMPED CIGAR BOX
  PURSE, p. 44
  A Lost Art
  Good Stamps Stamp Goods
  Stampa Rosa
  Stampers Anonymous
  Tin Can Mail

SILK SHAWL, p. 46
  Hero Arts
  JudiKins
  Rubber Gems
  Tin Can Mail

STAMPED CANVAS SHOES, p. 48
  Simply Stamps (Plaid)
  Sisters on Sojourn

STAMPED SILK TIE, p. 50
  100 Proof Press

STAMPED SUEDE CARRYING TUBE, p. 52
  Toybox

SAINT ALEGRÍA SHAWL, p. 54
  hand-carved stamps and alphabets
  Stamp Out Cute alphabet

FOR THE JEWEL BOX

WOODEN "PLAY" BROOCH, p. 58
  Burnt Offerings

DOMINO BRACELET, p. 60
  Acey Deucy
  Artifacts
  Limited Edition
  A Stamp in the Hand

"THOUGHT GIRL" NECKLACE, p. 62
  Limited Edition

SOLDERED ART CHARM JEWELRY, p. 64
  Acey Deucy
  Creative Block

"HOT!" STAMPED & BEADED BROOCH, p. 66
  Emerald City
  Viva Las Vegas Stamps

ETCHED METAL GODDESS BRACELET, p. 68
  Burnt Offerings

PINK BIRD NECKLACE, p. 70
  Suze Weinburg

ACKNOWLEDGMENTS

Thank you to every one of the artists who contributed art to this book. Without them, it wouldn't exist. Their hard work and cheerful cooperation made this project much easier, and their willingness to share their work is an inspiration to artists everywhere.

A special thank you to Anne Sagor. Not only does she create marvelous work, but she's fast and thorough and precise. Her extra hours made it possible for me to meet the early deadlines, and her proofreading and fact-checking skills from a former life as an English teacher were invaluable.

I'd also like to thank:

Sharilyn Miller, the author of the two previous rubber-stamping books by Rockport, who gave me her blessing and encouragement on this third volume.

Rachel Alverdin and Shirley Stephenson, the massage therapists whose hands undo all the damage done by too many hours at the keyboard.

Roberta, Michael, and Art at *Rubberstampmadness*, who have given me a writing home for the past dozen years and have provided me with the opportunity to meet fabulous artists like those featured in this book.

And, as always, my husband, Earl. For more than twenty-five years, he's provided the perfect environment—one of security and love and adventure—that every writer and artist needs in order to create. He offers ideas and inspiration and cheerfully attends conventions, art shows, estate sales, and flea markets. All of that, and he's cute, too.

ABOUT THE AUTHOR

Ricë Freeman-Zachery was teaching college English classes when, in 1992, she began writing regularly for *Rubberstampmadness*, the original rubber-stamp magazine. Since then she has written for *Art Dall Quarterly, Belle Armoire, Cat Fancy, Legacy, Personal Journaling, Somerset Studio,* and the *Studio.* Her projects and articles have also been featured in several books by Publications International, Ltd.

Her art—jewelry and dolls, handmade books, and bags—has been featured in galleries and shops from New Orleans and Santa Fe to Seattle and Tacoma. She teaches a variety of wearable art workshops.